The
KAROO
Cookbook

The Great Karoo – endless, dry, fascinating – patiently waits to be explored and enjoyed.

Dedicated to Wally – always the wind beneath my wings

COMPILED BY ROSE WILLIS • PHOTOGRAPHY BY RYNO

ACKNOWLEDGEMENTS

I would like to thank Joy Clack, Linda de Villiers and Beverley Dodd for holding my hand throughout this project, which wasn't without its difficulties. I also wish to thank Myrna Robins, food editor and author, who recommended me to Struik to write this book, as well as my sister Deanise Edwards, a home economics teacher and a pillar of strength, who helped and guided me where I was in doubt. And thank you, too, to the rest of my family, who have all been most supportive throughout and to all those who so willingly contributed.

ROSE WILLIS (JUNE 2008)

The publishers and contributors would like to thank the ICA for testing all the recipes.

INSTITUTE OF CULINARY ARTS

Pebbles and stubby bushes stretch as far as the eye can see to mountains that reach for the sky.

Struik Lifestyle
(an imprint of Random House Struik (Pty) Ltd)
Company Reg. No. 1966/003153/07
80 McKenzie Street, Cape Town 8001
PO Box 1144, Cape Town, 8000, South Africa

www.randomstruik.co.za

First published in 2008 by Struik Publishers
Reprinted in 2009

Copyright © in published edition: Random House Struik (Pty) Ltd 2008
Copyright © in text: Rose Willis 2008
Copyright © in food photographs: Ryno/IOA 2008
Copyright © in scenic photographs: Ryno 2008 except pages 74 (© Walter Knirr/IOA); 89, 137 (© Brent Naudé-Moseley/IOA); 139 (© Keith Young/IOA); 149 (© Steve Moseley/IOA)
Copyright © in map: Richard Mackintosh/IOA 2008

Reproduction: Hirt & Carter Cape (Pty) Ltd
Printing and binding: Craft Print International Pte Ltd, Singapore

PUBLISHER: Linda de Villiers
MANAGING EDITOR: Cecilia Barfield
EDITOR: Joy Clack
DESIGNER: Beverley Dodd
PHOTOGRAPHER: Ryno
STYLIST: Brita du Plessis
STYLIST'S ASSISTANT: Jennifer du Plessis
ILLUSTRATOR: Richard Mackintosh

ISBN 978-1-77007-610-5

www.imagesofafrica.co.za
IMAGES OF AFRICA
PHOTO LIBRARY

Over 40 000 unique African images available to purchase from our image bank at **www.imagesofafrica.co.za**

Contents

Karoo Cuisine

A fascinating blend of foods, feasts, flavours and festivals

Fascinating food is a feature of the Karoo. Everything from aardvark to zebra has made it into cooking pots and onto dinner plates. Culinary concoctions in this limitless land, where meat is spiced on the hoof, are delicious to some, repellant to others, but all prove that Karoo cuisine is as diverse as the area itself.

In South Africa the Karoo, a natural wonder and one of the world's unique arid zones, stands alone. Globally it's an envied rarity, researched by archaeologists, anthropologists, botanists, ecologists, geologists, palaeontologists and other scientists. This ancient semi-desert area, which lies on the largest plateau of its kind outside Asia, covers approximately 35 per cent of South Africa's land surface and straddles four of the country's nine provinces – the Western Cape, Northern Cape, Eastern Cape and Free State. Climate and biology separate this vast area into the massive Nama or Great Karoo; the Succulent Karoo, an ecological area including Namaqualand; the Tankwa Karoo, between the Cederberg and the Roggeveld Escarpment with the Ceres Karoo at its southern section; the Worcester-Robertson Karoo; and the Klein Karoo.

The history of this ancient world stretches across the millennia. Rich fossil beds spanning approximately 600 million years prove the existence of the Gondwana supercontinent and set it apart from any other place on earth. Yet the secrets of the Karoo's prehistory have not yet been fully revealed and from time to time exciting new discoveries stir the interests of palaeontologists from across the world.

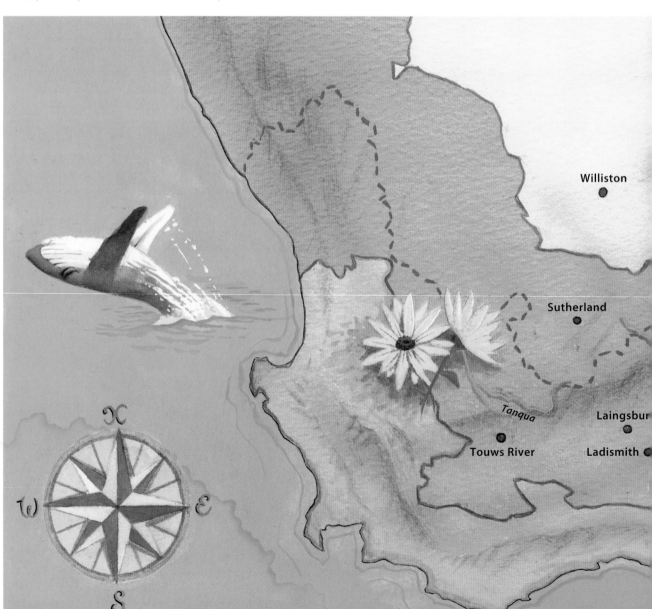

The Karoo harbours the largest variety of succulents found anywhere on earth. This desert flora is the richest in the world and 40 percent of the species are not found anywhere else. The Succulent Karoo has about 5 000 species and the Nama Karoo 2 200 – more than is found in the whole of Great Britain. Over the years many of these plants have also found their way into cooking pots and medicine chests.

The Karoo also has a rich human record. People have continuously inhabited the area for about 100 000 years, yet Early Stone Age tools near some drainage courses suggest intermittent occupation for over a million years. Some of the world's most important archaeological sites are found in the Central Karoo, which is home to some of the oldest Stone Age sites in South Africa. Traces of animal bones and plants at some sites have led archaeologists to exciting discoveries regarding the diet of ancient hunter-gatherers. Accounts of seventeenth to nineteenth century travellers also reveal much about food. Some found water so brackish and salty that even the horses would not drink it. John

Barrow, private secretary to Governor Lord MacCartney, writes of water 'salty as brine', and a river, Stinkfontein, 'saline to the taste' and with 'a disgusting fetid smell'. Some travellers mention a powdery, salt-like substance 'lying like snow on the ground'.

Adulphe Delegorgue, a French naturalist, who came to South Africa in the 1830s 'armed with elephant gun, enquiring mind and keen sense of humour', found the Karoo trying. When a field cornet invited him to join a group going to 'the northern most limits of the Colony', he excitedly accepted despite the fact that he was not used to daily riding. Overnighting on farms, they pursued a 'painful course' across the Karoo. 'The sun, combined with saline dust, affected my eyes. I could not keep them open. We found dry rivers, salty springs, scrawny vegetation and poor, but honest farmers. The water was too brack to drink, yet they made tea which they served without sugar. Taken hot, it tasted like medicine, but quenched the thirst.'

In the late 1700s Barrow enjoyed 'a kitchen garden plant' called 'mountain spinach'. Ornithologist François

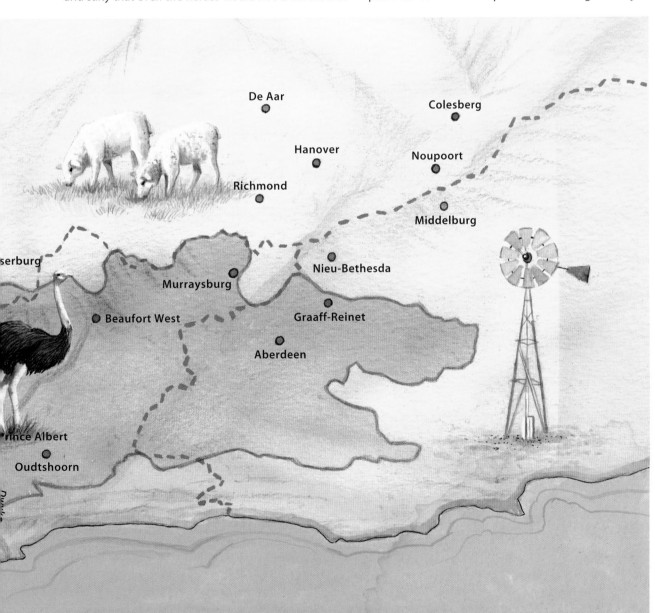

A lonely shepherd's hut against a typical Karoo backdrop.

le Vaillant, who kept a baboon, Kees, to taste his food, made fricassees of guinea fowl and partridge. He admired the beautiful touraco, or loerie, found only in the George-Plettenberg Bay area, but nevertheless caught them (and flycatchers) to cook. He claimed this fricassee was 'superior to guinea fowl or partridge with the same sauce'. Le Vaillant also mentions a yellowwood tree with a large plum-like fruit covered with small tubercles. Only the extremely hard kernel was edible. He writes of a red wood with fruit the size of an olive, but pleasurable to eat. Locals 'made spirituous liquors from it'. Experts say South Africa has no 'red wood' tree and that neither *rooi els* nor *rooi karee* trees have fruit matching his description.

Carl Peter Thunberg, a Swedish plant and animal collector, discovered a small, wild cucumber 'eagerly eaten' by Khoi and sheep. The colonists pickled it in vinegar, 'but it tasted very bitter'. He found a fungus-like plant near Calvinia, which small animals devoured and the Khoi considered a delicacy. Marloth called this *bobbejaankos* (baboon food), explaining it was a root parasite on euphorbias, with fruit that ripened underground. This *Hydnora* is the only known plant that produces woody flowers.

Early indigenous inhabitants lived on roots, leaves, wild plants, grass seeds, locusts, gum, river fish, reptiles, ant larvae (which colonists called Bushman rice), ostrich and tortoise eggs, and occasionally a bit of antelope meat. The settlers, however, treated themselves to more exotic titbits, including aardvark, porcupine, hare, hedgehog and tortoise. Today these taste treats of the old wagon route could never be considered as most of the animals are endangered and protected. One early delicacy, the small, nocturnal riverine rabbit (*Bunolagus monticularis*), is threatened with extinction. Old-timers regularly made a homely hotpot from this creature, which gastronomes knew as a *doekvoethaas* (cloth-foot rabbit), because of its large feet, or *pondhaas* (pound rabbit), because mature animals, when skinned and ready for the pot, usually weighed a pound.

Rich, nourishing tortoise eggs were a gastronomic treat. Clanwilliam-born author, poet, naturalist, doctor, epicurean and chef, C Louis Leipoldt, recommended tortoise soup as a tonic. These creatures fed on veld herbs and were considered flavoursome and 'tender as chicken'. Catching them was easy. They were not fleet-footed enough to flee. Their heads were cut off, and they were placed on the coals in their shells, round-side down and slowly baked. When done, the shell was cracked and the succulent meat scooped out. Hedgehogs were covered with a layer of muddy clay and baked in the embers until done. A smart tap cracked the clay, which fell away, prickles and all, leaving a feast of tender, tasty meat.

Peter Kolbe, an early German traveller, claimed the timid aardvark made superb eating. 'They have excellent hearing so are quick and difficult to catch, but those who've eaten them, salted or smoked, say their flesh is loaded with fat and delicious.'

Putting a porcupine on the menu required a bit of planning and a fair amount of courage. Author Lawrence Green said: 'They're rodents and they know how to defend themselves.' He warned that digging a porcupine out of its lair was no easy task, yet added they were not difficult to cook. 'They weigh about 27 kilograms on average, so, there's bound to be enough for everyone.' Preparing a porcupine for the pot also required effort. Once the quills were removed, the body had to be scalded and scraped to remove the hair. The flesh was then well washed to ensure no 'scrapings' landed in the pot. Porcupine apparently tasted like pork, but the 'crackling' was said to be much better. Food connoisseurs considered the skin a great delicacy, particularly when grilled over the coals and served with lemon butter.

In *The Emigrant's Cabin*, Thomas Pringle, also known as the 'father of South African poetry', pays tribute to the food of the Karoo:

'Pardon me for seeming somewhat rude, In this wild place how manage ye for food? … You'll find, my friend, we do not starve, There's always mutton, if nought else, to carve … on broad-tailed mutton, small and fine … for ten days we dine. Next roasted springbok, spiced and larded well, a haunch of hartebeest … a paauw … beats turkey hollow; korhaan, guinea fowl and pheasant follow … smoked ham of porcupine and tongue of gnu … fine household bread … comes from an oven too.' Then, he adds: 'Well, my friend, your dinner's good; springbok and porcupine are dainty food … the wildish flavour's not unpleasant; and may I say the same of gnu and pheasant.' He also mentions other delicacies, such as brawn of forest boar, green roasted maize, pumpkin pie, wild asparagus, grapes, figs, almonds, raisins, peaches and watermelon that, like sugared ices, melts in the mouth.

One mouthwatering veld plant was *kambro* (*Fockea edulis*), or *gambro*, a favourite of indigenous inhabitants and settlers. This ancient, edible tuber, which can weigh up to 50 kg, looks like a sweet potato and has flesh that tastes 'like spring water on a hot, dry, dusty day'. San women grated the tuber and mixed it with the ground dried seeds of the karee tree. Leipoldt described *kambro* as 'the white watery gold of the Karoo' and recommended that the best way to enjoy its unique flavour was to cook it with wild fennel, bay leaf and a touch of lemon rind. A 91-cm-long *kambro*, 45 cm in diameter, was served at a dinner for Cecil John Rhodes and other dignitaries, all of whom apparently enjoyed it. *Kambro*, they say, causes severe headaches and singing in the ears if eaten as the main source of food in winter. Mostly it was boiled in a sweet, sugary syrup to make delicious *kambrokonfyt*. The San feasted on it for years but, once the settlers discovered its taste, it became almost extinct. Today the plant is protected.

While *kambro* is a distant memory, several other unusual delicacies can still be found along the byways of the Karoo. One is *pofadder* (puff adder), not a snake as the name suggests, but a special sausage made from liver, kidneys and selected offal, minced with fat, flavoured with spices and traditionally stuffed into intestines for braaiing or pan-frying. *Muise* (mice), *vlermuise* (bats), *skilpadjies* (tortoises) or *wolfies* (wolves) may not sound appetizing, but they're truly delicious little sausages or parcels made from diced meat or liver enclosed in caul fat and braaied over the coals. Caul fat, the white lacy fat around the stomach and entrails of pigs, sheep and game, has been part of Karoo cuisine for years. The Khoisan named the Karoo's driest area around Leeu Gamka Koup, or Ghoup, because its sparse golden grass interspersed with brown earth patches reminded them of caul fat.

Pioneer farmers moving inland in search of grazing brought all food, apart from meat, with them. In this harsh hinterland they cooked in iron pots over open fires and recipe books were useless. Vegetables were unobtainable, so they relied on veld herbs for flavour. Thunberg found people enjoying the corm of the *Iris edulis* (now known as *Moraea edulis*, the *wituintjie*). When boiled, he said, it tasted just like potato. He also reported that anise root tasted good when roasted or boiled in milk. He mentions a 'most fragrant indigenous waterlily-like plant', *waterblommetjie* (*Aponogeton distachyos*), was a favourite for stews. It still is.

At each outspan along the wagon route, a basic soupy stew, *galopsop* (gallop soup), was prepared from each day's freshly slaughtered meat or venison. As the stew cooked, a bread dough was made, cut into thin strips called *skuinskoek*, and fried in hard fat. When done, this bread, a side dish to the stew, was spread with soft fat. An Irish priest, Rev. James O'Haire, who travelled the hinterland from 1863 to 1875, remembered meals of salty mutton washed down by brackish, almost muddy water. 'We gave our horses the best food we could and for ourselves cooked humble dinners of mutton or buck, boiled, roasted or toasted over the flames on a green stick.'

A Karoo farm boy, who qualified as one of South Africa's first veterinary surgeons, was 'filled with nostalgia' by memories of ox wagon trips. In *From the Horse's Mouth*, S W J van Rensburg says they travelled by wagon after their horses were commandeered during the Anglo-Boer War. 'There's a romance to this mode of travel. Produce for the market, wool, hides, skins, grain, butter, eggs and vegetables were loaded at the front. Adults sat on stretchers, which doubled as beds, in the shade of the canopy at the back while children skipped along outside. The oxen plodded on at three to four kilometres an hour, but never in the heat of the day. We

Tweedside Lodge, Matjiesfontein

set off in the late afternoon, outspanned at midnight to cook porridge, braai meat, tell ghost stories around the fires and then sleep for two or three hours. In the cool, pre-dawn we inspanned and lumbered off again until the heat compelled us to stop.'

Author Lawrence Green said that one of the finest meals he'd ever eaten came out of a three-legged pot in the Karoo. 'It was a *kelkiewyn* [Namaqua sandgrouse] stew that had simmered gently all day.' German doctor, explorer and epicurean Martin Karl Heinrich Lichtenstein, who travelled widely in the hinterland, enjoyed 'very agreeable repasts' in the Karoo, among them slivers of raw eland on bread and butter, and a *pens en pootjie* (stomach and trotter) stew. Hunter Cornwallis Harris also considered eland excellent. 'It melts in the mouth and, the brisket, is a cut for a monarch.'

Lichtenstein often started his day with a strong soup made from 'fowls, mutton or veal'. Lawrence Green once breakfasted on 'hot springbok fry, followed by cold springbok haunch, cold korhaan, steaming coffee with goat's milk, boermeal cookies, thinly planed springbok biltong, wild honey, stewed peaches, tomato and lettuce'.

Author Eve Palmer says there's no better epicurean delight than a breakfast of hard-boiled ostrich egg mashed with butter, pepper and salt and eaten piping hot on fresh farm bread. One ostrich egg equals about 24 chicken eggs and takes at least an hour to become hard boiled, yet this is a favourite dish in the Karoo. Experts say the Khoisan also enjoyed ostrich egg. They pierced the shell, scrambled the contents and placed the egg on a smouldering fire, or made an 'omelette' by pouring the egg straight onto coals. Once cooked, the 'omelette' was lifted, dusted off and shared out. Pickled ostrich egg is a delicacy today.

Way back, the main meal was served at midday. Lichtenstein mentions eating roast sucking pig, turkey and haunch of game, accompanied by six or eight sorts of preserved fruit. Chicken and pigeon pasties followed, plus a fruit pudding or milk tart. Karoo people loved melons, watermelons, grapes, mulberries, peaches, apricots, pomegranates, oranges, figs, almonds and other nuts. Early Beaufort Westers planted pear, peach and mulberry trees on their pavements. This so impressed one visitor that he wrote of beautiful clear nights filled with the scent of the pear blossom, which at times became quite 'fragrantly overpowering'. In 1994 a Loxton farmer rediscovered an old apple tree planted by his grandfather in 1899 and re-established this Sweet Sinclair so as to re-create Grandma's apple pie. Eve Palmer mentions 20 different apple varieties grown on Cranmere and 'magical sugared violets, a Christmas speciality, painstakingly made and packed in air-tight containers'.

Citrus grows well in the Karoo. When Hendrik Antonie Lodewijk Hamelberg passed through Beaufort West in 1856 he called the Karoo 'the land where the citrus blooms'.

Not all people, however, were complimentary. Some periodicals warned that life in the hinterland was 'far from luxurious'. Would-be travellers were told to expect 'rough and ready manners and a liberal, but coarse, bill of fare'. Hotels at remote outspans were likely to be corrugated iron structures, which would overheat stifling guests in summer and freeze them to death in winter. Individual beds were luxuries seldom encountered. The discovery of gold and diamonds in the interior forced landlords to attend to comfort and reasonable inns sprang up, but there were still no guarantees as far as food was concerned. 'Food along coach routes varies greatly. Meat is abundant, but inferior. Vegetables are few and fruit is always excessively dear,' wrote one journalist.

Generally the more remote the spot, the warmer the hospitality, said missionary minister Rev. B F G Bastiaans. He found many a hearty meal in the Karoo. Bastiaans had no transport. Cars were scarce, so he borrowed horses, mules, donkey carts or bicycles, but in the long run he found Shank's Pony the most reliable way to reach his far-flung flock. 'After each service I was treated to a sumptuous meal, mostly served on a tin plate which I balanced on my knees. The meal normally started with *roosterbrood*, hot from the coals and spread with goat's milk butter. Then followed a scrumptious rib stew flavoured with veld herbs. An enamel mug of coffee and goat's milk rounded off the meal. There was never any sugar to sweeten it.' Bastiaans planned each trip carefully to ensure he would always have water. 'Windmills were scarce and to safely travel in the Karoo one had to know where the fountains were.'

T C Lucas, a British soldier who came to South Africa 'to fight in Frontier Wars where one neither lived, nor died like a gentleman', loved Karoo food, but bedding, in his opinion left a lot to be desired. 'Farms beds are square platforms with huge feather mattresses that seldom smell sweet, nor do "feldt comberse", or quilts, which apparently are never washed, but, the food is tasty,' he wrote. 'It's mostly roasted or boiled meat with rice and raisins. Little "commitjies", or bowls of milk, are placed beside each person in the absence of liquor. Some farmers offer a kind of bitter "maag beer", which they drink before dinner. This is the only kind of fermented drink I ever saw in their houses, with the exception of a coarse spirit termed "Bucca Brandy", made from the seeds of a bush with the same name.' The most disagreeable part of the meal was swarms of flies. 'These flocked from all quarters and almost ate us alive.' He explained that to keep the herds from straying, or being stolen, farmers built cattle *kraals* (thorny enclosures) near their front doors. 'These attract the small pertinacious kraal fly. Food brings them indoors where each darts his proboscis into your flesh leaving an irritating little sting. These flies cover the meat and commit suicide in the milk by the hundreds. They are perfect pests. In better homes servants brush them away with chowries.'

Food has always set the social scene in the Karoo. It was a treat, a reward, a way to welcome guests and bid friends farewell. Central to culture, traditions and customs, it comforted the bereaved and helped spread joy at weddings and baptisms. Weddings were the best, wrote 'BA' in 1859's *The Cape Monthly Magazine*. 'Nothing on earth equals the excitement of a Karoo wedding. The atmosphere is electric as the host welcomes each horse and cart. All young men are ushered to an outbuilding to spruce up. (Damsels do this indoors.) The lads are given a basin, a jug of water, and a solitary comb, which they share. Each man steps up to the basin, completes his toilet, dries off with a communal towel, then checks his appearance in a fractured mirror and spits on his palms to smooth his hair to fashionable sleekness.

'People gather in small groups until the parson has done his bit. Then, they move to a large woolshed or barn where tables groan under a feast of venison, poultry, mutton and peacock – an unequalled delicacy of the Karoo. Tempting side and sweet dishes are irresistible. Convivial speeches follow this surfeit of food and allow the lads a closer look at the lasses. It becomes apparent many have made an attentive study of the fashion pages of the *Illustrated London News*. At the first squeak of a violin chairs and tables are swept aside and virtually everyone takes to the dance floor. Karoo lads, despite their heavy boots, are extremely agile. They rush to partner solid sylphs and nymphs of impressive girth, who too are light of heel and heart. Staid, old men puff rhythmically at their pipes talking of wool and weather, while mothers' eyes never leave the dancers, constantly checking that their daughters' honour is not besmirched and keenly scouting out suitable son-in-law material.' BA and his friends departed at four in the morning after a most enjoyable time. Their cart overturned en route home and slid down an embankment. Sunrise found them with 'unaccountable splitting headaches', which they blamed on a horse that lost its footing.

Such social occasions turned pioneer women into perfect bakers. They used flour supplied by mills, turned by hand, donkeys or horses in small towns and on farms. One Richmond mill, hundreds of kilometres from the sea, was constructed from pieces of a wrecked ship. Today, like the restored, water-driven mill at Prince Albert, it is a tourist attraction. The San also 'baked'. They made cookies from roasted, ground-up locusts mixed with honey. The paste, shaped into 'biscuits', was 'baked' or dried out on sun-drenched rocks. Myth, magic and superstitions surrounded honey, a delicacy, food and medicine. It was used to make a nourishing drink and a highly intoxicating beer.

Many veld herbs were also used as medicine and in cooking. Buchu, named by the Khoi and considered a wonder herb, grows in many places. At least 13 species grow in the Swartberg Mountains near Prince Albert. Indigenous people used dried leaves in wedding rituals and mixed these with sheep fat to make a 'skin moisturiser'. Early travellers sent samples abroad and there medical men praised its properties. Buchu was a vital component of Grandma's medicine chest and Grandpa relied on buchu brandy for his medicinal needs. Buchu vinegar added a unique taste to cooking. The classic, medicinal buchus are fynbos shrubs of the citrus family (Rutaceae), rather than Succulent Karoo or Nama Karoo plants. Aromatic shrubs of the daisy family (Asteraceae), Genus *Pteronia*, occur widely within the Karoo and have names like *boegoebossie* and *boegoekaroo*. These were widely used as body perfumes by the Khoisan.

Wine was essential and served at most meals to 'wash down' the food because milk, when available, was for children. Looking at the excellent products available throughout the region today, one would imagine that everyone enjoyed winemaking. But this was not so. Some missionaries, like Erasmus Smit, were quite literally driven to drink trying to teach their flock to make wine. Today wines and ports are world class and the *witblitz* (white lightning) is internationally known. It's used as a medicine and in cooking. Some say there's nothing to touch the stuff stoked in Die Hel, or Gamkaskloof as residents prefer to call it. Others firmly believe the Klaarstroom version owns the magic, while yet others prefer the bottled bliss from Fransie Pienaar Museum in Prince Albert. But, no matter where it's from, experts agree *witblitz* will cure whatever ails you and a good dollop in a stewpot will do wonders for the flavour. *Witblitz* is an excellent flambé.

Karoo brandies were powerful. Robert Gray, the first Bishop of Cape Town, found Beaufort West's best brandy almost magical. He once was handed a bottle, which he stuck into his saddlebag. En route home his horse took a bad turn and collapsed at an isolated spot. The bishop feared the horse would die, so poured some brandy down its throat and over its nostrils. At first there was no response, then to his delight the horse stood up and trotted merrily along next to him with 'a new lease on life'.

In the Karoo, horizons are infinite and footprints few.

The earliest settlers drank tea made from infusions of dried leaves from veld plants. They enjoyed these concoctions weak and without milk. Coffee was an 'import'. The *trekboers* drank a concoction called *gaat*, made from an infusion of shepherd's (*witgat*) tree the roots. *Smouse* (pedlars), who brought almost everything to the Karoo, also brought the coffee. When supplies ran out weird blends were developed by grinding dried carrots, ripe figs, peach pips, prickly pear peels, peas or mealies to a powder. Some of these brews had distinctive flavours. Mealie coffee was a favourite of Boer commandos during the Anglo-Boer War. Their coffee not only warmed them, but it kept them well. Experts say that Boer soldiers did not contract typhoid (enteric fever) because they boiled water to make coffee, whereas British soldiers often filled their water bottles from polluted rivers and streams.

In 1904 a pedlar let down Beaufort West shopkeeper Isadore Bakst, who needed pepper. Bakst came up with what he considered a solution. He ground olive pips to a fine powder and 'extended' his pepper supplies. This landed him in court where he was fined 40 shillings.

Karoo cuisine has a rich heritage of culture, history and traditions. Mutton, venison and fruits carry the Karoo's name beyond South Africa's borders. Wines and ports are internationally acclaimed. Beef, poultry and pork ring the changes in the kitchen, while venison and ostrich keep waistlines trim.

Discover the towns of the vast Karoo

There are about 80 towns, villages, little hamlets and settlements within the huge expansive area known as the Karoo. Each has its own story and taste treats.

In the Northern Cape are: Britstown, Calvinia, Campbell, Carnarvon, Colesberg, De Aar, Douglas, Fraserburg, Griquatown, Hanover, Hopetown, Hutchinson, Marydale, Loxton, Orania, Petrusville, Philipstown, Prieska, Richmond, Sutherland, Strydenburg, Victoria West, Vosburg and Williston.

In the Eastern Cape are: Aberdeen, Cookhouse, Cradock, Graaff-Reinet, Hofmeyr, Jansenville, Klipplaat, Middelburg, Nieu-Bethesda, Noupoort, Norvalspont, Pearston, Rietbron, Steytlerville, Somerset East (bordering on the Midlands), Steynsburg, Venterstad and Willowmore.

In the Western Cape are: Beaufort West, Ceres, Klaarstroom, Laingsburg, Leeu-Gamka, Matjiesfontein, Merweville, Murraysburg, Nelspoort, Prince Albert, Prince Albert Road, Touws River, Three Sisters, the Tanqua-Karoo, as well as the Vleiland and Rouxpos settlements towards Seweweekspoort.

The Klein Karoo (also part of the Western Cape): Amaleinstein, Barrydale, Calitzdorp, De Rust, Dysselsdorp, Haarlem, Ladismith, Montagu, Oudtshoorn, Schoemanshoek, Uniondale, Vanwyksdorp and Zoar.

Soup played a pivotal role in history

In the Karoo soup is more than just a comfort food for cold winter nights. It's an integral part of hinterland hospitality and a meal in its own right, not simply a starter to stimulate the appetite. Traditionally, huge black enamel soup pots burbled almost permanently at the edge of coal stoves, with hearty broth always ready to welcome unexpected guests. Soup served in the Karoo also played a pivotal role in South African history: it made a poor railwayman wealthy and it 'toppled' a government. James Douglas Logan, the Scot who owned Matjiesfontein, rocketed from a poor porter to one of South Africa's richest men, all thanks to soup. Rail travellers, desiring a meal at his station restaurant, had to order and pay in advance. Apparently the soup was served so hot that it could not be eaten before the train whistle blew and travellers were forced to dash off, leaving the rest of the meal untouched. Later, Logan's Railway Food Concession indirectly caused the collapse of Cecil John Rhodes's government, but that's another tale. Modern-day Matjiesfontein has certainly not lost its touch for the extra hot – chilli sherry is a speciality. A 'wee dram' certainly gets the circulation going, and a good splash picks up a bowl of soup in a most lively way. A hot red chilli in each bottle ensures its magic never fails.

The gateway to the Tanqua-Karoo near Ceres, one of the region's original routes into the hinterland.

Soups and Starters

CREAM OF SPINACH SOUP WITH HERBED CROUTONS

2 kg fresh spinach, well washed, ribs and
stalks removed, and chopped
500 ml (2 cups) milk
30 ml (2 Tbsp) butter
1 onion, grated
30 ml (2 Tbsp) cornflour
5 ml (1 tsp) salt
1 ml (¼ tsp) freshly ground black pepper
50 ml (just over 3 Tbsp) fresh cream

HERBED CROUTONS
4 slices slightly stale bread
Butter for spreading
Salt and freshly ground black pepper
Chopped fresh herbs of choice
A little mustard powder

Note: To make a delicious bread salad, add
the croutons to 250 ml (1 cup) crisply fried,
crumbled bacon, 100 ml (a bit under ½ cup)
mayonnaise and 25 ml (5 tsp) sour cream.
Toss to coat, check seasoning. Serve on
washed and dried lettuce leaves.

Place the spinach in a large saucepan and cook slowly until tender (do not add water, there will be sufficient on the freshly washed leaves). Liquidize the cooked spinach in a food processor or press through a sieve. Warm the milk in a separate saucepan. Melt the butter in the saucepan in which the soup is to be cooked. Sauté the onion until translucent. Gently stir in the cornflour, salt and pepper and stir continuously to ensure no lumps form. Slowly add the warmed milk, continuing to stir until the mixture thickens. Add the processed spinach. Stir well and heat through, but do not boil. Adjust the seasoning. Stir in the cream just before serving hot with herbed croutons. **SERVES 4–6**

Herbed croutons: Preheat the oven to 180 °C. Remove the crusts from the bread. Thinly spread both sides of each slice with butter. Cut each slice into 1-cm cubes and place these on a baking sheet. Sprinkle with salt and pepper and some dried or chopped fresh herbs and spices of your choice, plus a little mustard powder if you like. Toss lightly to ensure even coverage. Bake for 20–25 minutes until golden brown. Turn regularly using a spatula or egg lifter and periodically shake the baking sheet to prevent burning. Cool.

SWEET POTATO AND LENTIL SOUP

30 ml (2 Tbsp) olive oil
1 onion, peeled and finely chopped
1 kg sweet potatoes, washed, peeled and
cut into cubes
1.25 litres (5 cups) chicken stock
45 ml (3 Tbsp) tomato purée
250 ml (1 cup) red lentils
2.5 ml (½ tsp) ground cumin
Salt and freshly ground black pepper to taste
250 ml (1 cup) flaked cooked chicken
(optional)
Fresh cream and chives for garnishing

Heat the oil in a soup pot and gently fry the onion until translucent. Add the sweet potatoes and stir well. Add chicken stock, tomato purée, lentils, cumin and seasoning. Simmer for 30 minutes until the sweet potatoes are cooked. Cool and liquidize. Add the flaked chicken if using. Reheat before serving. Garnish with a swirl of cream and finely chopped chives. **SERVES 4–6**

Note: Lentil soup was on the menu at a dinner given in 1845 by Christina, wife of Voortrekker leader Andries Pretorius. She also served bobotie, rissoles, sliced green beans, potatoes, cauliflower, larded venison, mutton, chicken, turkey, cold tongue, ham, salads and small sandwiches. The meal was rounded off by a dessert of *pannekoek* (pancakes) and waffles, writes Elria Wessels in *Boerespyse*.

Sweet Potato and Lentil Soup

BEAN SOUP

500 g sugar beans
3.5 litres Rooibos tea for soaking beans
1 litre chicken stock
150 g bacon, chopped
1 large onion, roughly chopped
2 large potatoes, peeled and grated
2 medium tomatoes, skinned and chopped
2 large carrots, washed, peeled and grated
1 large stick celery, grated
Salt and freshly ground black pepper to taste
Grated Cheddar cheese and cayenne pepper
for garnishing

Wash the beans and place in a glass bowl. Add the Rooibos tea, cover and soak overnight.

Next morning: Place the beans and tea into a soup pot, add the chicken stock and slowly bring to the boil. Simmer until the beans are cooked. In a separate pan, sauté the bacon and onion for a few minutes, and then add to the soup mixture. Add the rest of the vegetables and seasoning and simmer gently for 30–45 minutes until done. Serve as chunky soup, garnished with grated Cheddar cheese and a sprinkling of cayenne pepper. **MAKES ABOUT 4 LITRES**

Note: Beef shin can also be used to make the stock for this delicious bean soup. Choose bones with good marrow centres. When the marrow has cooked, carefully remove the bones from the soup pot and slide the cooked marrow onto slivers of toast. Serve as a side dish with a dusting of salt and pepper.

Bean Soup

BEETROOT SOUP

STOCK

1 kg pork short rib
2 onions, chopped
1 large stick celery, chopped
4 sprigs parsley, chopped
2 carrots, chopped
6 peppercorns
2 bay leaves
5 ml (1 tsp) chopped fresh thyme or 1 ml dried thyme
4 litres water

Simmer all the stock ingredients together for 2 hours until the meat falls easily from the bones. Remove the bones and whole spices. Liquidize. Then add:

750 g beetroot, grated
375 ml (1½ cups) sliced onion
250 ml (1 cup) chopped celery
2 tomatoes, skinned and chopped
25 ml (5 tsp) wine vinegar
12.5 ml (2½ tsp) salt
5 ml (1 tsp) chopped fresh dill
2.5 ml (½ tsp) freshly ground black pepper
500 ml (2 cups) sliced cabbage
125 ml (½ cup) grated potatoes
2 large potatoes, cubed
80 ml (⅓ cup) chopped fresh parsley

Simmer gently for about 45 minutes, or until done. Garnish with a swirl of sour cream and serve. **MAKES ABOUT 4 LITRES**

Note: This soup freezes well.

CARROT SOUP

25 ml (5 tsp) butter or 30 ml (2 Tbsp) oil
1 onion, chopped
3 cloves garlic, chopped
4 cm piece fresh ginger, peeled and grated
5 carrots, peeled and diced
1 medium sweet potato, peeled and diced
10–12 soft dried apricots, chopped
1.5 litres chicken stock
Salt and freshly ground black pepper to taste
Fresh cream, toasted flaked almonds and chopped
    fresh parsley for garnishing

Heat the butter or oil in a large saucepan and sauté the onion, garlic and ginger for a few minutes. Add the carrots, sweet potato, apricots, chicken stock, salt and pepper and simmer for 30 minutes. Allow to cool and then blend in a food processor, or blitz with a hand mixer until smooth.

To serve: Gently reheat the soup, taking care not to let it burn. Garnish with a swirl of cream, toasted flaked almonds and chopped parsley. **SERVES 4–6**

A cheeky boer goat enjoys a snack.

Weed Soup à la Crème

Well-known author, poet and epicurean C Louis Leipoldt maintained 'anything can go into the soup pot'. Prince Albert's Mary Sandrock agrees. She recently astonished local residents, who'd been complaining of a winter opslag (influx) of weeds, by telling them to make soup. She then gave them her recipe for **Cream of Weed Soup**. *'You need to go about in your garden and collect all the greens you can find: wild mustard, nettles, sorrel, dandelions, wild spinach, purselaine, borage, comfrey and calendula leaves, as well as beetroot and turnip tops. Wash the leaves well and place them in a large pot with a little water and a pinch of bicarb to preserve a good green colour. Then boil quickly and allow to cool. Liquidize and freeze in 500 ml containers. When you want to prepare the soup, make a litre of thick white sauce, add the liquidized weeds, season and dilute to the consistency you require with some chicken stock. Bring to the boil. Season with lemon pepper, rosemary and olive or garlic salt. Serve with a swirl of cream or yoghurt and a sprinkle of chopped parsley or yellow calendula petals.' Those who tried it all agreed it was delicious.*

    Note: *Mary also makes a delicious* **Cream of Artichoke Soup** *in a similar way. 'Scrub Jerusalem artichoke bulbs well, but do not peel them,' she says. 'Cut them into chunks and place these into a saucepan with sufficient water to just cover them. Boil until soft, liquidize and freeze. When needed, make this into a soup by adding the artichoke base to a litre of thick white sauce. Dilute with chicken stock, bring to the boil, season and serve.'*

ONION TART

CRUST	
250 ml (1 cup) cake flour	
5 ml (1 tsp) baking powder	
Salt	
60 ml (4 Tbsp) butter	
60 ml (¼ cup) hot water	

Crust: Sift the flour, baking powder and salt together. Make a hollow in the centre. Melt the butter in the hot water and pour into the hollow. Then gently work the liquid into the dry ingredients until the dough leaves the sides of the bowl. Spoon the dough into an ovenproof pie dish and press out along the bottom and up the sides.

FILLING	
2–3 hard-boiled eggs	
50 g butter	
1 medium onion, finely chopped	
30 ml (2 Tbsp) cake flour	
500 ml (2 cups) milk	
1 egg	
150 ml (just over ½ cup) grated Cheddar cheese	

Filling: Preheat the oven to 180 °C. Slice the hard-boiled eggs and place a layer across the bottom of the uncooked pastry. Melt the butter in a saucepan and sauté the onion until translucent. Add the flour and stir, taking care not to let it form lumps. Slowly add the milk, beaten egg and cheese. Pour the mixture into the pie crust and bake for 40 minutes, or until set and golden brown on top. **MAKES 10–12 SLICES**

IVER PÂTÉ

500 g lamb's or calf's liver, cleaned
and chopped
3 rashers bacon, crisply fried and crumbled
250 ml (1 cup) white sauce
1 onion
1 clove garlic
1 medium red pepper, cored and de-seeded
1 small can anchovy fillets
3 eggs, lightly beaten
15 ml (1 Tbsp) prepared English mustard
65 ml (just over ¼ cup) fresh cream
Salt and freshly ground black pepper to taste

Preheat the oven to 160 °C. Grease a 750 ml ovenproof dish. Sauté the liver until no longer bloody, then drain and cool. While the liver is cooling, fry bacon and make the white sauce. Mince together the cooled liver, onion, garlic, red pepper, and anchovy fillets using the mincer's fine blade. Place the mixture in a bowl, and then add the eggs, mustard, cream, bacon and the white sauce. Mix well and season to taste. Spoon into the prepared greased dish. Place this dish in an oven pan with sufficient water to reach halfway up the sides. Bake on the middle shelf of the oven for about 1 hour, or until a knife inserted in the centre comes out clean. Cool and refrigerate for at least 24 hours before serving. This will allow the flavours to develop fully. **MAKES 750 ML**

Liver Pâté

MAKE-IN-THE-DISH QUICHE

PASTRY BASE

30 ml (2 Tbsp) oil

125 ml (½ cup) milk

300 ml (1¼ cups) cake flour

2.5 ml (½ tsp) salt

ASPARAGUS AND CHEESE FILLING

1 x 475 g can asparagus tips, drained

250 ml (1 cup) grated mature Cheddar cheese

2 eggs

250 ml (1 cup) milk

2.5 ml (½ tsp) cayenne pepper

2.5 ml (½ tsp) salt

15 ml (1 Tbsp) butter to dot on top

MUSHROOM AND CHEESE FILLING

10 ml (2 tsp) olive oil

30 ml (2 Tbsp) finely chopped onion

1 clove garlic, finely chopped

30 ml (2 Tbsp) chopped bacon

375 ml (1½ cups) button mushrooms, wiped clean and sliced

15 ml (1 Tbsp) brandy

2.5 ml (½ tsp) chopped fresh thyme

15 ml (1 Tbsp) chopped fresh parsley

Salt and freshly ground black pepper to taste

1 egg

125 ml (½ cup) milk

125 ml (½ cup) grated Cheddar cheese

30 ml (2 Tbsp) smooth cream cheese

Pastry base: Preheat the oven to 180 °C and place an oven tray in the oven to heat up. Mix the oil and milk together in a measuring cup. Sift the flour and salt directly into an ovenproof 23 cm pie dish. Make a hollow in the centre of the dry ingredients and pour in the oil and milk mixture. Stir gently until a dough is formed. Press this out evenly in the pie dish. Pour in the filling of your choice and place the dish on the preheated tray. Bake for 30–35 minutes, or until set and the base is golden brown.
MAKES 10–12 SLICES

Asparagus and cheese filling: Arrange the asparagus tips over the uncooked pastry shell. Mix all the other ingredients, except the butter, together and pour over the asparagus. Dot butter on top. Bake for 30–35 minutes, or until set and the base is golden brown.

Mushroom and cheese filling: Heat the olive oil in a large frying pan and sauté the onion and garlic until translucent. Add the bacon and fry for a few minutes. Add mushrooms, brandy, thyme, parsley and seasoning. Stir-fry briskly for a few minutes, then remove from heat and allow to cool. Do not overcook. Beat the egg, add milk, cheese and cream cheese together and fold this mixture into the mushroom mixture. Pour into the uncooked pastry shell and bake for 30–35 minutes, or until set and the base is golden brown.

Note: This quick and easy pie can be whipped up in minutes for lunch, supper or as a treat for unexpected guests. It lends itself to virtually any filling, i.e. egg and bacon, cheese and vegetables, chicken and mushroom, spinach and feta, and so on. It is an excellent way to use up leftovers in an interesting way.

Make-in-the-dish Quiche with Asparagus and Cheese Filling

A small flock of sheep on a quiet stretch of road in the Fraserburg-Loxton area.

Meat

Lamb and Mutton

Spiced on the hoof, it's the gourmet's choice

World-famous Karoo lamb graces homely dinners and formal banquets. Master chefs agree there's nothing to beat it. In 1999 South African chefs took 'Laingsburg Lamb' to the International Chefs Olympiad in Luxembourg, convinced its 'uniquely different flavour' would give them the edge. And it did! Judges relished the distinctive character of their dishes, and most were intrigued by the extra hint of flavour in the meat itself. Some say this comes from the scrubby Karoo bushes that the sheep eat as they browse across the arid veld; others claim it's a mix of *karoobossie* and grass, while yet others maintain the region's brackish water does the trick. No-one has ever discovered the secret and a select group even attributes the flavour to the general ambience and tranquillity of the Karoo. This, they say, prevents animals from becoming stressed and so contributes to the tenderness and taste of the meat. 'Who cares,' says a top chef. 'I've never discovered the secret, but my palate knows the difference.' Most international tourists agree. Almost all make a point of trying lamb or mutton in its 'home environment'. The not-so-adventurous choose rosemary as flavouring, but epicureans love to explore exotic flavours, like lamb with lavender, preserved ginger or black pepper crusting. They're also easily tempted to try offal, *stertjies* (docked tails) or *peertjies* (testes), which connoisseurs say are unequalled when curried. Early cookery books are crammed with recipes proving mutton was a perpetual favourite. In *Return to Camdeboo*, Eve Palmer says her brother called it '365 meat' because it was eaten almost every day! Many others write of traditional dishes, such as de-boned leg of lamb larded with garlic and stuffed with dried fruit and fresh garden herbs. When slow-cooked overnight in a damped-down coal stove oven its tempting, mouthwatering aromas crept into every room in the house from the early hours.

Mutton Neck Roll

1 mutton neck (± 1.5 kg), de-boned and butterflied
Preserved apricots for garnishing

FILLING
1 bunch spinach leaves, washed and stalks and ribs removed
10 ml (2 tsp) olive oil
1 large onion, chopped
15 ml (1 Tbsp) chopped olives
30 ml (2 Tbsp) crumbled feta cheese
30 ml (2 Tbsp) fresh breadcrumbs
1 egg, beaten
Gelatine
Wine vinegar
Salt and freshly ground black pepper to taste
Ground coriander to taste

Preheat the oven to 180 °C. Cook the spinach in a large pot without adding any water. Cool and chop. Heat the olive oil in a saucepan and fry the onion until softened. Place in a bowl, add the chopped olives, spinach, feta cheese, breadcrumbs and egg and mix well. Flatten the butterflied neck and sprinkle with gelatine. Pile the filling on top of this and sprinkle some more gelatine over the filling. Roll the meat up tightly and secure with string. Sprinkle with wine vinegar, salt, pepper and coriander. Place on a greased oven tray and bake for about 1 hour, or until tender. Garnish with preserved apricots. **SERVES 4–6**

LAMB WITH DATES AND HONEY

1.5 kg shoulder of lamb, trimmed and cubed

2.5 ml (½ tsp) salt

2.5 ml (½ tsp) freshly ground black pepper

15 ml (1 Tbsp) cake flour

60 g butter

2 onions, roughly chopped

500 ml (2 cups) beef stock

1 cinnamon stick

10 ml (2 tsp) honey

5 ml (1 tsp) ground cinnamon

2 cloves garlic, finely chopped

2.5 ml (½ tsp) dried sage

250 g (1 packet) pitted dates, chopped

Season the meat with the salt and pepper. Sprinkle lightly with flour and toss to coat. Melt the butter in a saucepan and sauté the onions until translucent. Add the meat and fry until nicely browned. Add the stock and the cinnamon stick and bring to the boil. Simmer for 1½ hours, or until the lamb is tender. Using a slotted spoon, remove the meat and set aside. Remove the cinnamon stick and discard. Stir in honey, ground cinnamon, garlic and sage. Simmer gently for 10–15 minutes, allowing the flavours to develop. Return the meat to the saucepan, add the dates, stir well and cover. Simmer for a further 10 minutes, or until the dates are plump and the sauce coats the meat (it may be necessary to thicken the sauce with a little cornflour). Serve hot on a bed of rice and with a green salad. **SERVES 4–6**

Lamb with Dates and Honey

Karoo Lamb Shanks with Creamy Samp

KAROO LAMB SHANKS WITH CREAMY SAMP

1.5 kg lamb shanks
15 ml (1 Tbsp) chopped fresh rosemary
2 large leeks, roughly chopped
Dried peel from ¼ naartjie
2 large carrots, roughly chopped
1 apple or quince, cored and roughly chopped
50 ml (just over 3 Tbsp) balsamic vinegar
250 ml (1 cup) water
750 ml (3 cups/1 bottle) red wine
10 ml (2 tsp) coarse salt
Freshly ground black pepper to taste
1 x 410 g can red kidney beans
Cornflour for thickening

CREAMY SAMP (*MIELIERYS*)
250 ml (1 cup) samp
500 ml (2 cups) fresh cream
1 sprig fresh rosemary
25 ml (5 tsp) butter
Salt and freshly ground black pepper to taste

Preheat the oven to 160 °C. Place all the ingredients, except the red kidney beans and cornflour, in a casserole and season with salt and pepper. Cook slowly for 4 hours or longer, until tender. Add the red kidney beans and thicken the sauce with a little cornflour. Serve with creamy samp (below). **SERVES 4–6**

Creamy samp: Soak the samp in water for about 3 hours. Drain. Cook in fresh water until just soft. Add the cream and rosemary. Cook for a few more minutes so that the rosemary flavour can develop. Add butter and season to taste. Leave to stand for 5–10 minutes to allow the samp to absorb the cream and thicken.

CORIANDER LAMB

15 ml (1 Tbsp) olive oil
1 large onion, chopped
600 g stewing lamb, cut into cubes
Salt and freshly ground black pepper to taste
3 cloves garlic, crushed
30 ml (2 Tbsp) chopped fresh parsley
250 ml (1 cup) water
5 ml (1 tsp) cornflour, mixed with a little water to make a paste
500 ml (2 cups) plain yoghurt
5 ml (1 tsp) grated lemon peel
30 ml (2 Tbsp) finely chopped fresh coriander leaves

Heat the oil in a large, deep frying pan and sauté the onion until translucent. Add the lamb and brown. Add salt, pepper, garlic and parsley, stir well and cook for a minute or two. Add the water, cover and simmer until the lamb is tender – about 1½ hours. Stir in the cornflour and yoghurt. Add the lemon peel. Finally add the finely chopped coriander and simmer gently for 5–10 minutes. Do not boil as the mixture may curdle. Serve hot with cooked brown rice. **SERVES 4–6**

$\mathscr{M}$UTTON BREDIE WITH DRIED FRUIT

375 ml (1½ cups) dried sugar beans
250 ml (1 cup) samp
250 ml (1 cup) dried apple rings or dried
apricots (or a combination of both)
125 ml (½ cup) sultanas
1.5 kg mutton, cut into cubes
3 onions, chopped
Seasoned flour for coating
30 ml (2 Tbsp) oil
30 ml (2 Tbsp) curry powder
15 ml (1 Tbsp) sugar
20 ml (4 tsp) brown vinegar
60 ml (¼ cup) water
A little cornflour to thicken

The day before: Soak the sugar beans and samp in water overnight.

Next day: Chop the dried fruit and place with the sultanas in a bowl of water to soak. Drain the beans and samp, place in a saucepan with fresh water to cover and boil until soft.

Mix the meat and onions together and sprinkle with seasoned flour, then shake off excess. Heat the oil in a saucepan and brown the meat and onion mixture in small batches. Take care not to let it burn. When all the meat has browned, add it to the cooked samp and sugar bean mixture with 1 litre of water and simmer slowly for about 2 hours until meat is tender. Mix together the curry powder, sugar, vinegar and 60 ml water and add to the bredie with the dried fruit. Simmer slowly for a further 10 minutes to allow the flavours to develop. Add cornflour to thicken, if necessary. **SERVES 4–6**

$\mathscr{Q}$UICK AND EASY MUTTON STEW

2 kg stewing mutton
25 ml (5 tsp) oil
1 large onion, roughly chopped
250 ml (1 cup) water
Salt and freshly ground black pepper to taste

SAUCE
50 ml (just over 3 Tbsp) brown onion
soup powder
50 ml (just over 3 Tbsp) gravy powder
50 ml (just over 3 Tbsp) tomato sauce
50 ml (just over 3 Tbsp) oxtail soup powder
50 ml (just over 3 Tbsp) fruit chutney
12.5 ml (2½ tsp) vinegar

Cut the meat into cubes. Heat a little oil in a flat-bottomed pot and sauté the onion. Add the meat and brown slightly. Add the water and season with salt and pepper. Cover and bring to the boil. Simmer for 2–3 hours, or until the meat is tender, checking from time to time that the stew does not become dry. Mix all sauce ingredients with a little water and add to the meat mixture. Gently bring to the boil and cook until the sauce thickens. **SERVES 4–6**

Mutton Bredie with Dried Fruit

TRIPE WITH LEMON JUICE AND CUMIN

About 750 g sheep's tripe, rinsed in cold water
with 15 ml (1 Tbsp) lemon juice
15 ml (1 Tbsp) olive oil
1 large onion, finely chopped
2–3 cloves of garlic, crushed
1 chilli, de-seeded and chopped (optional)
5 ml (1 tsp) salt
5 ml (1 tsp) ground cumin
5 ml (1 tsp) vinegar
15 ml (1 Tbsp) lemon juice
125 ml (½ cup) grated Cheddar cheese
5–6 medium potatoes, peeled and cut into matchstick-size chips
1 good handful of fresh parsley, chopped

Place the tripe in a saucepan and bring to the boil. Boil for about 1 hour or until just tender. Heat the oil and sauté the onion, garlic and chilli until just soft. Drain the tripe and cut it into thin strips. Add and fry until the moisture in the pan reduces. Add salt, cumin, vinegar and lemon juice and stir well. Add the cheese. Stir well. Fry the potato chips until crisp. Add the parsley and chips to the tripe and stir. Serve hot. **SERVES 6–8**

Note: When the meat is cut into such small slivers most people cannot believe that they are eating tripe. Dr Heinrich Lichtenstein came across *pens en pootjies* (tripe and trotters) for the first time in his life on a trip into the interior. He was more than impressed with the clean and hygienic way in which the housewives prepared this dish.

CURRIED BRAWN

1 sheep's head and trotters or 12 trotters
Salt and freshly ground black pepper
15 ml (1 Tbsp) medium curry powder
60 ml (¼ cup) vinegar
12 peppercorns
15 ml (1 Tbsp) coriander seeds
12 whole allspice/pimento berries
4 bay leaves
4 whole cloves
Grated peel of 1 lemon

Clean the sheep's head and trotters. Chop into pieces, place in a heavy-based saucepan and cover with cold water. Bring to the boil and simmer gently for 2–3 hours until the meat is tender. Add salt, pepper, curry powder and vinegar. Tie all the other spices, plus the lemon peel, into a cheesecloth bag and add to the meat mixture. Cook for 30 minutes until the meat falls from the bones. Cool. Remove the bones and the bag of spices. Flake the meat and return it to the pot. Reheat and spoon into moulds or glass dishes. Refrigerate until set. **SERVES 8–10**

Boepensie — A Favourite of Yesteryear

1 sheep's reticulum (honeycomb stomach), cleaned

STUFFING
1 onion, finely chopped
2 lamb's kidneys, membrane and core removed, minced
1 mutton liver, minced
125 ml (½ cup) pork crackling
5 ml (1 tsp) grated nutmeg
15 ml (1 Tbsp) brown vinegar
125 ml (½ cup) sultanas
15 ml (1 Tbsp) cake flour

Combine all ingredients for the stuffing. Stuff the reticulum with the mixture and sew up the opening. Place in a large saucepan and cover with water. Bring to the boil and simmer until cooked. Cool.

SAUCE
15 ml (1 Tbsp) butter
1 onion, sliced
500 ml (2 cups) boiling water
25 ml (5 tsp) brown vinegar
25 ml (5 tsp) sugar
25 ml (5 tsp) apricot jam
Salt and freshly ground black pepper to taste
25 ml (5 tsp) cake flour

To make the sauce, melt the butter and sauté the onion until softened. Add the boiling water, vinegar, sugar and jam and season with salt and pepper. Bring to the boil, thicken with flour and cook a little longer. Slice the boepensie thinly and serve with the hot sauce. Serves 4–6

LUCERNE BREDIE

60 ml (4 Tbsp) cake flour
10 ml (2 tsp) chopped fresh thyme
5 ml (1 tsp) salt
2.5 ml (½ tsp) freshly ground black pepper
1 kg stewing mutton, cut into cubes
25 ml (5 tsp) olive oil
2 onions, roughly chopped
2 cloves garlic, finely chopped
4 medium potatoes, peeled and cubed
2 x 500 ml (2 cups) lucerne tops
Grated peel of 1 lemon
25 ml (5 tsp) tomato sauce
A few drops of Worcestershire sauce

Mix the flour, thyme, salt and pepper and toss the meat in this mixture, making sure that it is evenly covered. Heat the oil in a saucepan. Brown the meat in batches. Remove from the pan and drain well. Add the onions and garlic to the pan and fry until translucent. Return the meat to the pot and add 15 ml (1 Tbsp) water and potatoes. Reduce the heat and simmer for about 1 hour, or until the meat is tender. Add the lucerne and simmer until cooked. Stir in the remaining ingredients and simmer for a few minutes more. Serve on samp or with mashed potatoes. **SERVES 4–6**

Note: Spinach can be used in this dish if preferred, or if lucerne is not available.

Curried Testes – A Tradition of the Sheep Farms

On every sheep farm, a day or two was set aside each year to mark new lambs, dock their tails and castrate extraneous rams. 'Cruel as this may sound, this is the only way to ensure a top quality breeding programme,' says ecologist and historian Pat Marincowitz. 'In days of yore one worker had a small enamel bowl to catch the testes, or peertjies as they were called. Removal was easy: the 'cutter' merely grabbed the points of the testes with his front teeth, bit down and pulled them out. This hurt the lambs much less than cutting them and trying to remove the testes with the fingers. Back at the farmhouse peertjie kerrie was cooked by placing the testes in a large pot with vinegar, salt, pepper and curry powder. When ready, the mixture was turned out into a bowl and left to stand overnight to set. The result was a dish that tasted like marrow or brains. There were no tough sinews and it was absolutely delicious.' When tail docking began, farm children quickly made a fire nearby to braai the docked tails. The woolly skins were pulled off and children and workers alike enjoyed these crispy morsels straight from the coals. 'We grew up secure in the knowledge that these dishes were fit for a king – true koningskos,' says Pat.

A passing shower has left welcome pools of water along a rural road.

OUMA'S KAROO LAMB PIE WITH SOUR CREAM PASTRY

2 kg stewing mutton or a mixture of shoulder,
neck and knuckles, cut into small pieces
(do not remove the bones)
10 ml (2 tsp) salt
2.5 ml (½ tsp) freshly ground black pepper
Flour for dusting meat
20 ml (4 tsp) olive oil
1 onion, finely chopped
1 bay leaf
5 whole cloves
5 peppercorns
500 ml (2 cups) chicken stock
5 ml (1 tsp) ground coriander
2.5 ml (½ tsp) grated nutmeg
2.5 ml (½ tsp) cayenne pepper
10 ml (2 tsp) mustard powder
2 cloves garlic, finely chopped
10 ml (2 tsp) brown sugar
60 ml (¼ cup) brown vinegar
A little cornflour mixed to a paste with cold
water for thickening

SOUR CREAM PASTRY
750 ml (3 cups) self-raising flour
5 ml (1 tsp) salt
250 g ice-cold butter
20 ml (4 tsp) brandy
250 ml (1 cup) sour cream

Season the meat with the salt and pepper, and dust with a little flour. Heat the oil in a saucepan and brown the meat. Add the onion, bay leaf, cloves and peppercorns and stir-fry gently for a few minutes. Add the chicken stock and simmer gently for 2 hours until the meat falls from the bones. Allow to cool. When cool, remove the bones, gristle, bay leaf, peppercorns and cloves. Flake the meat. Return the meat and liquid to the saucepan, add the rest of the spices, and the garlic, sugar and vinegar and bring to the boil. Simmer for 5 minutes. Adjust the seasoning and thicken with a little cornflour if needed – a fairly 'gluey' mixture is needed for this pie. Spoon the mixture into an ovenproof pie dish and place a pie funnel or up-turned egg cup in the centre to prevent the pastry from sagging and becoming soggy. Cover with Sour Cream Pastry (below) and bake for about 25 minutes at 180 °C until the pastry is flaky and golden brown. **SERVES 4–6**

Note: Preferably use mutton and not lamb for this dish, as the flavour is richer. If possible use a combination of meats such as neck, shoulder and shank (make sure that the shank bones are sawn through so that the marrow can escape and add to the hearty richness of the dish). Do not remove the bones until the mixture has cooled. This ensures a good flavour.

Sour cream pastry: Sift the flour and salt into a large bowl. Working quickly and lightly, cut the butter into small 1-cm cubes. Toss into the flour. Stir the brandy into the sour cream and add all at once. Cut the mixture with a knife until it forms a dough. Knead the dough into a ball. Cover and refrigerate for about 30 minutes. Roll out on a floured board to about 1 cm thick. Fold in half and in half again to form a square. Turn this square anti-clockwise until the next side faces you and roll out again. Fold up once more. Repeat this rolling and folding process twice more (so that the dough has been rolled 4 times in total). Then, finally fold the dough into a square, cover and refrigerate for 30 minutes. Roll out and use.

Note: This pastry, which will make two shells for covering with a mashed potato topping, or one pie with a pastry top, will keep well in the refrigerator for 2 or 3 days.

Ouma's Karoo Lamb Pie with Sour Cream Pastry

Goat

Healthy and deliciously different

Goat is an essential part of Karoo cuisine. Often overlooked, it is a healthy source of protein and is low in fat and cholesterol. Braaied, stewed, roasted or curried it rings the changes on any menu in a most interesting way. Goat meat is delicious cooked with dried fruit such as peaches, apricots, prunes, raisins, sultanas or apple rings, fresh herbs and spices. Kid's meat is an essential part of New Year celebrations in the Eastern Cape Karoo region, where loin pie is a delicacy and roast stuffed leg a taste treat on the festive table.

GLAZED GOAT LEG WITH PINEAPPLE

1 x 2 kg leg of goat, de-boned
10 ml (2 tsp) salt
Freshly ground black pepper to taste
1 x 480g can pineapple rings, drained
(reserve the juice)
Butter for frying
4–5 glacé cherries for garnishing

STUFFING
500 ml (2 cups) fresh breadcrumbs
50 ml (just over 3 Tbsp) chicken stock
1 large onion, finely chopped
125 ml (½ cup) chopped walnuts
100 g button mushrooms, wiped clean
and chopped
60 ml (4 Tbsp) finely chopped fresh parsley
1 canned pineapple ring, finely chopped
1 egg, beaten
2.5 ml (½ tsp) salt
Freshly ground black pepper to taste

GLAZE
45 ml (3 Tbsp) chicken stock
15 ml (1 Tbsp) prepared English mustard
15 ml (1 Tbsp) honey
15 ml (1 Tbsp) brandy
15 ml (1 Tbsp) pineapple juice (reserved from
the can of pineapples)
A little chicken stock and cornflour dissolved
in water for making the gravy

Preheat the oven to 180 °C.

Stuffing: Mix all ingredients for the stuffing until well combined. Season the meat on both sides and place the stuffing in its centre. Roll up and tie with string. Place the meat, fat side up, on a rack in a roasting pan, add 125 ml (½ cup) water and roast in the oven for 30–40 minutes, or until the meat is tender. While the meat is roasting in the oven, prepare the glaze.

Glaze: Heat the chicken stock and stir in the other ingredients. Simmer gently for a minute or two. Remove from heat. Using a pastry brush, paint the glaze onto the roast at regular intervals while it is in the oven. At the end of the cooking period, when the meat is removed from the oven, paint it once more, then set the meat aside to rest for at least 10 minutes before carving. Add leftover glaze to the pan juices with some chicken stock to make the gravy. Thicken the gravy with a little cornflour dissolved in cold water.

To garnish: Fry the pineapple rings in butter until golden and place on the leg with a glacé cherry in the centre of each.
SERVES 6–8

SMOKED LEG OF BOERBOK (BILLY GOAT)

1 x leg of boerbok (about 2 kg)

BRINE
5 litres water
1 kg salt
250 g brown sugar
10 g saltpetre
5 g bicarbonate of soda
10 g mixed pickling spices of choice

Mix all the ingredients for the brine together in a saucepan and bring to the boil. Simmer for 15 minutes, continuously removing any scum that rises to the surface. Set aside until cold. Place the boerbok leg into this brine and weigh it down. Cover it and leave for 10 days in a cool place – turn twice a day.

After 10 days remove the leg from the brine and pat dry. Place in a smoker and smoke overnight.

Place the leg into a large pot, cover with water and boil gently for 3–4 hours until done. Serve with mustard and slices of spanspek (sweet melon). **SERVES 4–6**

Note: Coriander seeds, whole cloves, pimento, peppercorns, peeled and chopped ginger, cinnamon sticks, bay leaves – tied in a muslin bag – are a good combination of pickling spices.

Glazed Goat Leg with Pineapple

Stuffed Belly of Pork with Peanut Butter Marinade

Pork

Set a new tone for high days and holidays

Over the years pork has set the tone for social events and festive occasions in the Karoo. Hot, heavy meals were a tradition at Christmas when roast pork and crackling was a treat, and anyone who could crisp crackling was respected. New breeding techniques and scientific feeding have made pork leaner. It's now lower in kilojoules and cholesterol, rich in Vitamin A, B, iron and calcium and recommended to dieters. Way back, sucking pig was also a traditional favourite, but fattening a porker was not without its terrors. In 1830 wild barking awoke a Kariega farmer. Afraid that someone might be out to steal his Christmas porker, he crept out to his kraal, but the night was moonless and he couldn't see anyone moving about. He peered into the darkness trying to see what had disturbed his dogs. Then, seeing what he thought to be his horse in front of him, he reached out to stroke its mane. To his horror he found he was touching an elephant. He turned and fled with the startled elephant in hot pursuit. In pitch darkness he raced towards his house, sheer terror guiding his feet and keeping him ahead. Dashing around the last corner he flew through his front door as the elephant shot by, so close on his heels that it knocked out some stones from the corner of the house. He heard it crash on through the brush and across the river. 'And thus disappeared the last Kariega elephant,' reported the local minister, Rev. E G Evans, the next day.

STUFFED BELLY OF PORK WITH PEANUT BUTTER MARINADE

1 x 2 kg belly of pork

MARINADE
30 ml (2 Tbsp) olive oil
125 ml (½ cup) peanut butter
300 ml (1¼ cups) tomato sauce
90 ml (6 Tbsp) Worcestershire sauce
2 cloves garlic, crushed
Salt and freshly ground black pepper to taste
60 ml (¼ cup) sherry

STUFFING
125 g (½ packet) dried apricots
60 ml (¼ cup) sherry
1 large onion, finely chopped
60 ml (4 Tbsp) finely chopped fresh parsley
5 ml (1 tsp) dried mixed herbs or 15 ml
(1 Tbsp) finely chopped fresh herbs of choice
125 ml (½ cup) oats
2 slices brown bread, crusts cut off, crumbed
1 egg
Salt and freshly ground black pepper to taste

Mix all the marinade ingredients and marinate the pork for at least 6 hours, but preferably overnight. Turn from time to time. Reserve the marinade.

Stuffing: Preheat the oven to 160 °C. Soak the apricots in the sherry for a few hours until plump. Mix all the stuffing ingredients together until well combined. Remove the pork from the marinade and spread out. Season with salt and pepper. Place the stuffing in the centre and roll up, tying tightly with string. Roast in the oven for about 2 hours, or until tender. Remove the pork. Skim the fat from the pan juices, add the leftover marinade and stir well. Bring to the boil and thicken with cornflour, if necessary. **SERVES 4–6**

STIR-FRIED ORANGE PORK

1 kg pork fillet, sliced and cut into thin strips

MARINADE
30 ml (2 Tbsp) orange juice
30 ml (2 Tbsp) lemon juice
10 ml (2 tsp) olive oil
5 ml (1 tsp) soy sauce

STIR-FRY MIX
20 ml (4 tsp) olive oil
1 medium onion, finely sliced
2 sticks celery, cut into thin strips
2 large carrots, julienned
250 g button mushrooms, wiped clean and sliced
1 leek, well washed and thinly sliced
1 yellow pepper, cored and de-seeded and cut into thin strips
4 cloves garlic, finely chopped
Salt and freshly ground black pepper to taste
15 ml (1 Tbsp) chopped fresh herbs of your choice (i.e. a mixture of parsley, sage and thyme)

Marinade: Place the pork strips in a bowl. Mix all the ingredients for the marinade and pour over the pork. Toss the meat in this mixture until it is well covered and set aside to marinate for a few hours in the refrigerator.

Stir-fry mix: Heat the oil in a wok or large pan. Sauté the onion until translucent. Drain the meat and add (reserve the leftover marinade). Fry the meat lightly for a few minutes. Add the celery, carrots, mushrooms, leek and pepper strips, and continue frying, stirring all the time. Add the garlic, stir well and continue frying until the vegetables are crisp and almost cooked. Turn up the heat, pour small amounts of the leftover marinade (to taste) into the pan and stir rapidly, so that it quickly evaporates, leaving only flavouring on the meat and vegetable mix. Remove from the heat before the vegetables become soft and soggy. Add seasoning and herbs. Serve immediately on rice or noodles. **SERVES 6**

Note: If only a hint of garlic is required, add the garlic at the beginning of the cooking process with the onions. If a stronger garlic flavour is required, stir it in at the end.

BAKED PORK CHOPS

15 ml (1 Tbsp) oil
1.5–2 kg pork chops
1 onion, chopped
2–3 cloves garlic
50 ml (just over 3 Tbsp) lemon juice
25 ml (5 tsp) vinegar
10 ml (2 tsp) brown sugar
45 ml (3 Tbsp) Worcestershire sauce
45 ml (3 Tbsp) tomato sauce
5 ml (1 tsp) prepared English mustard
Salt and freshly ground black pepper to taste
300 ml (1¼ cups) chicken stock
10 ml (2 tsp) cornflour

Preheat the oven to 160 °C. Heat the oil and fry the chops until golden brown, but not totally cooked. Drain. Place the chops in the bottom of a baking dish. Fry the onion until golden, add the garlic, and stir-fry lightly. Add all the other ingredients, stir well and bring to the boil. Pour this sauce over the chops. Cover the dish and bake in the oven for about 1 hour. Remove the cover and continue cooking until the meat is tender and browned. Serve with mashed potatoes and peas. **SERVES 8–10**

Stir-fried Orange Pork

Roast Pork Stuffed with Prunes

Roast Pork Stuffed with Prunes

About 15 large pitted prunes
125 ml (½ cup) good quality port
3 cloves garlic, finely chopped
30 ml (2 Tbsp) finely chopped fresh parsley
10 ml (2 tsp) mustard powder
50 ml (just over 3 Tbsp) dried breadcrumbs
20 ml (4 tsp) butter
1 x 2 kg leg of pork
Salt and freshly ground black pepper to taste
125 ml (½ cup) water

Note: Leftovers from this roast are delicious. Small chunks can be added to a green summer salad to turn it into a delicious lunchtime meal.

The day before: Place the prunes in a bowl, add the port and soak for a few hours until plump. In a separate bowl, mix the garlic, parsley, mustard and breadcrumbs with the butter to make a paste. Divide this mixture into 15 little balls and stuff each into the centre of a prune. Pack the prunes into a container and freeze. Reserve any leftover port to add to the gravy.

Next day: Preheat the oven to 180 °C. Trim the pork and score the rind if you want crackling. Make 15 deep incisions all over the pork and push a frozen, stuffed prune into each. Season the leg and place on a rack in a roasting pan. Add 125 ml (½ cup) water and roast for 1 hour. Reduce the heat to 160 °C and roast for a further 1½ hours, or until the meat is tender. Baste occasionally and add water to the roaster if necessary. When the meat is done, skim off any fat in the roasting dish, add the leftover port to the pan juices and make a gravy. **SERVES 6–8**

Spicy Pork Fillets with Plums and White Wine

750 g (3–4) pork fillets

MARINADE
2.5 ml (½ tsp) black peppercorns
15 ml (1 Tbsp) coriander seeds
10 ml (2 tsp) brown sugar
2 cloves garlic, crushed
30 ml (2 Tbsp) olive oil
30 ml (2 Tbsp) lime or 20 ml (4 tsp) lemon juice
60 ml (¼ cup) soy sauce

SAUCE
30 ml (2 Tbsp) butter
10 ml (2 tsp) brown sugar
125 ml (½ cup) fruity white wine
300 g firm sweet red plums, washed, halved and de-pipped (or 2 apples, cut into chunks)
30 ml (2 Tbsp) sunflower oil
15 ml (1 Tbsp) curry powder
10 ml (2 tsp) ground coriander
5 ml (1 tsp) ground ginger
250 g leeks, well washed and thinly sliced
4 sticks celery, thinly sliced
4 medium young carrots, julienned
125 ml (½ cup) chicken stock
Salt and freshly ground black pepper to taste

Trim the fillets (leave whole) and place in a flat glass dish.

Marinade: Using a mortar and pestle, crush the peppercorns, coriander seeds and sugar to a powder and sprinkle this over the pork. Toss to ensure that the mixture evenly covers the meat. Mix the garlic, oil, lime juice and soy sauce together and pour over the meat. Toss once again to ensure the meat is well covered. Set aside for 3–4 hours or place in the refrigerator overnight to allow the flavours to develop.

Sauce: Heat the butter in a saucepan, add the sugar and stir until melted. Add the wine, bring to the boil, and then add the plums. Cook for 2–3 minutes, and then transfer the plums and sauce into an ovenproof dish.

Preheat the oven to 160 °C. Remove the meat from the marinade (reserve the marinade). Heat the sunflower oil in a pan and brown the pork quickly to seal in the juices. Using a slotted spoon, remove the meat from the pan and add it to the plums in the ovenproof dish. Then, add the curry powder, coriander and ginger to the pan in which the meat was fried and stir-fry these spices lightly. Add the leeks, celery, carrots and leftover marinade and fry for a minute or so to bring out the flavours. Add this mixture to the pork and the plums. Add the chicken stock and place in the oven. Cook for 20–25 minutes until the meat is tender. Adjust seasoning. Serve on rice or noodles. **SERVES 6–8**

EASY BACON SUPPER DISH

30 ml (2 Tbsp) oil
250 g (1 packet) bacon, chopped
2 onions, finely chopped
3 sticks celery, finely sliced
2 carrots, peeled and grated
1 red pepper, cored and de-seeded
and finely sliced
5 ml (1 tsp) dried mixed herbs
Salt and freshly ground black pepper to taste
1 small cabbage, finely chopped
250 ml (1 cup) cake flour
250 ml (1 cup) milk
10 ml (2 tsp) curry powder
2 eggs, beaten
250 ml (1 cup) grated Cheddar cheese
Dried origanum to taste

Preheat the oven to 180 °C. Heat the oil in a large saucepan. Fry the bacon rapidly, and then add the onions and fry until softened. Add the celery, carrots, red pepper, mixed herbs, salt and pepper and stir-fry for 4–5 minutes. Add the cabbage and stir-fry for about 5 minutes. Cover the saucepan and simmer the mixture for about 4 minutes. Remove from the heat. Mix the flour, milk and curry to a paste and add the eggs. Add this to the cabbage mixture. Stir well. Place the mixture into a greased ovenproof dish. Sprinkle with cheese and origanum and bake for about 30 minutes until set. Serve hot or cold. **SERVES 8–10**

Note: To vary this dish, cook sufficient potatoes to make a mashed topping and mash them with milk, butter, salt and pepper. Add 2 more well-beaten eggs to the cabbage mixture and omit the flour. Spoon into a greased ovenproof dish and top with mash. Sprinkle cheese and origanum over this and bake at 180 °C for 30 minutes until golden brown on top.

THICK RIB WITH APPLE STUFFING

2 pieces (2 kg) de-boned pork thick (spare) rib
Salt and freshly ground black pepper to taste

MARINADE
125 ml (½ cup) soy sauce
60 ml (¼ cup) honey
30 ml (2 Tbsp) sherry
2 cloves garlic, crushed
10 ml (2 tsp) mustard powder
15 ml (1 Tbsp) lemon juice
5 ml (1 tsp) dried thyme

STUFFING
60 ml (4 Tbsp) butter
1 large onion, finely chopped
2 sticks celery, washed and finely chopped
2.5 ml (½ tsp) dried sage
2.5 ml (½ tsp) dried thyme
2.5 ml (½ tsp) dried marjoram
30 ml (2 Tbsp) finely chopped fresh parsley
1 cooking apple, peeled, cored and grated
60 ml (4 Tbsp) brown sugar
125 g toasted breadcrumbs
125 ml (½ cup) cooked brown rice
1 egg

Marinade: Score the crackling on both pieces of rib and place the meat in a bowl. Mix all ingredients for the marinade and pour over the meat, making sure both pieces are coated. Marinate for at least 2 hours, turning after 1 hour.

Stuffing: Preheat the oven to 180 °C. Remove the meat from the marinade and season. Reserve leftover marinade to use for basting. Heat the butter in a pan and sauté the onion, celery and dried herbs. Add the parsley and stir well. Remove from the heat and add the apple, sugar, breadcrumbs and rice. Beat the egg and add. Mix well. Adjust seasoning. Lay one piece of rib on a flat surface and evenly spread the stuffing over it. Cover with the second piece of rib, tucking the edges around the stuffing. Tie up tightly with string at regularly spaced intervals. Place the rib on a rack in a roasting pan, pour in 125 ml (½ cup) water and roast for 1½–2 hours, or until the meat is tender. To finish, carefully brown both sides under the grill. **SERVES 6–8**

PORK KNUCKLES WITH DILL

3 pork knuckles (eisbein)
25 ml (5 tsp) oil
3 small onions, chopped
3 large carrots, chopped
15 ml (1 Tbsp) dill seeds
4 whole allspice/pimento berries
1 stick celery, shredded into long strips
for garnishing
Salt to taste

Place the knuckles in a pressure cooker with a little water and steam for about 1½ hours. Remove from the heat and cool. Reserve the liquid. Remove the meat (which should be tender) from the bones and chop. Heat the oil in a separate saucepan and fry the onions. Add them to the liquid in which the pork was cooked. Add the carrots, dill, allspice and chopped pork and cook for about 30 minutes, uncovered, to allow the sauce to reduce and thicken. Check seasoning. Garnish with celery strips just before serving with rice and sauerkraut. **SERVES 6**

Agave aloes near Graaff-Reinet, the only place outside Mexico where this plant is used to distill a tequila-type liquor.

Beef Fillet with Anchovy Stuffing

Beef

Both medicine and hearty treat

Beef is one of the Karoo's traditional taste treats. Beef pot roast held pride of place on hinterland menus for years and was a speciality of many small hotels. But beef has also played an important role in medicine. Author, doctor, epicurean and chef C Louis Leipoldt used biltong – an absolute luxury today – as a medicine to treat duodenal ulcers. Years ago London hospitals ordered vast quantities of biltong for convalescent patients and Shackleton took hundreds of pounds with him to sustain his team as they crossed the ice of Antarctica. Biltong-making is said to have grown out of the practice of making tassels, a delicacy of the early Cape. Strips of meat were salted and peppered, laid in vinegar for a few weeks, then rinsed for pan-frying, wind-drying or *braaiing* (barbecuing). The practice is said to have found its way into the hinterland to become biltong, say some experts. Modern-day dieticians warn of the dangers of red meat, but Leipoldt said 'No matter what faddists may say meat, wine and oil could sustain the human body in perfect health.' Early travellers found hinterland beef inferior, stringy and tough, but it has improved since then and today tantalizing aromas and flavours of brown stews fill the air of many a Karoo kitchen. Beef *boerewors* (farmer's sausage) is another speciality of the Karoo. There are many recipes for wors, each containing special or secret ingredients, but they all add to the charm and enjoyment of Karoo cuisine.

BEEF FILLET WITH ANCHOVY STUFFING

1–1.5 kg beef fillet
15 ml (1 Tbsp) oil
30 ml (2 Tbsp) finely chopped bacon
3 onions, finely chopped
2 cloves garlic, crushed
1 x 45 g can anchovy fillets
2.5 ml (½ tsp) dried thyme
2.5 ml (½ tsp) dried sage
10 ml (2 tsp) chopped fresh parsley
10 ml (2 tsp) finely grated lemon peel
1 egg yolk
Freshly ground black pepper to taste

Preheat the oven to 220 °C. Cut a pocket into the fillet and set aside. Heat the oil and fry the bacon until crispy. Add the onion and garlic and continue frying until this is golden. Remove from the heat and cool. Soak the anchovies in milk for 10 minutes, then drain and chop. Mix the anchovies with the herbs, lemon peel, egg yolk and black pepper. Fill the pocket of the fillet with this mixture and fasten with toothpicks. Rub the fillet well with oil and place on a greased baking sheet. Cook for 10 minutes at 220 °C, then lower the temperature to 200 °C and cook for a further 10 minutes per 500 g of meat, turning halfway through the cooking process. Remove from the oven, cover lightly and leave the meat to rest for 10 minutes before slicing. **SERVES 6–8**

Note: Adjust the cooking time if you do not like the juices to run pink, i.e. 30–40 minutes will be rare and 50–60 minutes will ensure the fillet is well done.

BEEF TONGUE WITH RAISIN SAUCE

1 beef tongue
salt to taste

Place the tongue in a saucepan, cover with salted water and simmer until tender. Allow to cool, and then remove the skin, cut the tongue into slices and arrange loosely in an ovenproof dish.

SAUCE
150 ml (⅔ cup) brown sugar
5 ml (1 tsp) mustard powder
25 ml (5 tsp) cake flour
50 ml (just over 3 Tbsp) vinegar
50 ml (just over 3 Tbsp) lemon juice
12.5 ml (2½ tsp) grated lemon peel
375 ml (1½ cups) water
125 g (½ packet) seedless raisins

Sauce: Preheat the oven to 160 °C. Mix the sugar, mustard and flour together. Place in a saucepan and add the rest of the ingredients. Heat slowly, stirring continuously, until the mixture begins to boil and thicken. Pour the sauce over the tongue slices and place the dish in the oven to heat through before serving. **SERVES 4–6**

CORNED BEEF WITH MUSTARD SAUCE

2 kg corned beef
1 bay leaf
2.5 ml (½ tsp) peppercorns
1–2 whole cloves
Salt and freshly ground black pepper to taste

Place the beef in a saucepan, cover with cold water, add the remaining ingredients and bring to the boil. Simmer for about 1 hour, or until the meat is tender. Cool and slice.

SAUCE
1 x 480 g can pineapple pieces
25 ml (5 tsp) cornflour
25 ml (5 tsp) sugar
Salt and freshly ground black pepper to taste
10 red glacé cherries
75 ml (5 Tbsp) ready-made mild mustard or
(30–45 ml (2–3 Tbsp)) Dijon mustard

Sauce: Preheat the oven to 160 °C. Drain the pineapple pieces and chop finely. Reserve the juice and add water to make it up to 440 ml (1¾ cups). Pour into a saucepan and bring to the boil. Mix the cornflour, sugar, salt and pepper with a little water and add to the sauce. Cook until the sauce thickens and becomes shiny. Cut the cherries into quarters and add to the sauce. Stir in the chopped pineapple and mustard. Place layers of meat and sauce alternately into an ovenproof dish, ending with sauce. Place the dish into the oven for 10–15 minutes to heat through before serving. **SERVES 6–8**

Aberdeen's beautiful Post Office and Magistrates Court building, constructed from local sandstone, was completed in 1898.

Fruity Beef Casserole

FRUITY BEEF CASSEROLE

250 ml (1 cup) pitted prunes
250 ml (1 cup) dried apricots
250 ml (1 cup) water
30 ml (2 Tbsp) oil
1.5 kg lean beef, cut into cubes
2 onions, roughly chopped
1 tomato, skinned, de-seeded and chopped
37.5 ml (2½ Tbsp) brown sugar
25 ml (5 tsp) orange marmalade
12.5 ml (2½ tsp) brandy
Grated peel and juice of 1 lemon
4 whole cloves
2.5 ml (½ tsp) ground ginger
2.5 ml (½ tsp) ground cinnamon
2.5 ml (½ tsp) paprika
2.5 ml (½ tsp) Worcestershire sauce

The day before: Soak the prunes and apricots in the 250 ml (1 cup) water overnight.

Next day: Preheat the oven to 180° C. Heat the oil in a large, flat-bottomed saucepan and brown the beef in batches. Remove and place in a large casserole dish. Fry the onions and tomato in the pan in which the meat was browned. Add this mixture to the casserole. Add all the remaining ingredients, including the fruit and the water in which it was soaked, to the pan and bring to the boil, stirring well to loosen all the pan flavours. Pour this mixture over the meat in the casserole. Cover. Place the dish in the oven and cook for about 1 hour, or until the meat is tender. Check seasoning and thicken the sauce with cornflour if necessary. **SERVES 4–6**

BEEF STEW WITH SOUR CREAM AND CHILLI

2 kg stewing beef, cut into cubes
2 onions, coarsely grated
2 cloves garlic, chopped
2 green chillies, de-seeded and finely chopped
600 g button mushrooms, wiped clean and sliced
15 ml (1 Tbsp) cornflour
10 ml (2 tsp) mustard powder
625 ml (2½ cups) chicken stock
25 ml (5 tsp) soy sauce
100 ml (a bit under ½ cup) red wine
30 ml (2 Tbsp) oil
300 ml (1¼ cups) sour cream
Salt and freshly ground black pepper to taste

Place the meat in a large oven pan. Add the onions, garlic, chillies and mushrooms. Place the cornflour and mustard powder in a bowl, and add the chicken stock, soy sauce, red wine and oil, mixing well to ensure that there are no lumps. Pour this mixture over the meat. Stir well to ensure that the meat is well covered and set aside for at least 3 hours.

Preheat the oven to 180 °C. Cover the pan with foil, place in the oven and cook for 1–1½ hours, or until the meat is tender and brown and the sauce is thick. Remove from the oven and stir in the sour cream and seasoning. Return to the oven for 5 minutes, just to reheat. Do not allow the mixture to boil as it may curdle. **SERVES 6–8**

ONE-STEP BEEF CASSEROLE WITH RED WINE

500 g stewing beef, cut into cubes
2 large onions, chopped
3 pickling onions (press a few whole cloves into one)
2 bay leaves
250 ml (1 cup) chopped fresh parsley
15 ml (1 Tbsp) Worcestershire sauce
5 ml (1 tsp) salt
Freshly ground black pepper to taste
125 ml (½ cup) red wine
125 ml (½ cup) beef stock
30 ml (2 Tbsp) brandy
2 large carrots, diced
5 ml (1 tsp) dried thyme
1 slice brown bread, crumbed
30 ml (2 Tbsp) tomato paste
5 ml (1 tsp) sugar
250 g (1 punnet) button mushrooms, wiped clean
Additional 125 ml (½ cup) red wine
Triangles of toast and chopped parsley for garnishing (optional)

Preheat the oven to 160 °C. Place all the ingredients, except mushrooms, additional wine and the garnish, into a large casserole dish. Cover with a well-fitting lid and cook on the middle shelf of the oven for about 1¾ hours, or until the meat is tender. Stir in the mushrooms and extra red wine and cook for a further 45 minutes – by then the meat should be brown and the sauce thick. If the sauce has not thickened sufficiently, stir in a little cornflour that has been mixed to a paste with cold water. Remove the bay leaves and the onion with the cloves. Spoon into a serving dish and garnish with toast triangles and parsley. **SERVES 6–8**

Note: Bredies made with wine are normally tastier if made a day ahead and reheated. If you intend doing this, only thicken the sauce on the day that you reheat the dish.

SKILPAD (TORTOISE) OR MEATBALLS WITH SOUR CREAM

500 g beef mince
250 ml (1 cup) sour cream
1 packet oxtail soup powder
1 onion, grated

Preheat the oven to 180 °C. Mix all the ingredients together and shape into balls. Place in an ovenproof dish and bake in the oven for 30–35 minutes. Served with mashed potatoes. **SERVES 4–6**

Note: These meatballs are also delicious served cold.

One-Step Beef Casserole with Red Wine

Curried Banana Frikkadels

CURRIED BANANA FRIKKADELS (MEATBALLS)

5 slices white bread
150 ml (just under ⅔ cup) water or meat stock
cubes dissolved in water
1 kg beef mince
2 eggs
2.5 ml (½ tsp) grated nutmeg
2.5 ml (½ tsp) ground cloves
Salt and freshly ground black pepper to taste
Cake flour for coating

SAUCE
20 ml (4 tsp) butter
4 medium onions, grated
50 ml (just over 3 Tbsp) cake flour
125 ml (½ cup) vinegar
500 ml (2 cups) water
37.5 ml (2½ Tbsp) curry powder
25 ml (5 tsp) turmeric
75 ml (5 Tbsp) smooth apricot jam
50 ml (just over 3 Tbsp) sugar
Salt and freshly ground black pepper to taste
12 bananas

Soak the bread in the water or stock and then stir it into the mince. Add the eggs and seasonings and mix well. Shape into balls, roll in flour, shake off excess and pack loosely into a baking dish.

Sauce: Preheat the oven to 180 °C. Melt the butter in a pan and fry the onions until lightly browned. Add the flour and slowly stir in the vinegar and water. Add the curry powder, turmeric, jam, sugar, salt and black pepper and six of the bananas (sliced). Simmer until the bananas are soft. Slice the rest of the bananas and arrange the pieces among the meatballs. Pour the sauce over and bake in the oven for 40–45 minutes until the meatballs are cooked. Serve on a bed of rice. **SERVES 8–10**

TASTY ALL-IN-ONE MINCE SUPPER DISH

10 ml (2 tsp) olive oil
1 kg beef mince
2 large onions, chopped
1 tomato, skinned, de-seeded and chopped
Salt and freshly ground black pepper to taste
Chutney to taste
500 ml (2 cups) uncooked rice
1 x 285 g can mushrooms, plain or creamed,
as preferred
1 brinjal (aubergine), peeled and thinly sliced
6 pattypans, washed and thinly sliced
4 baby marrows (courgettes), washed and
thinly sliced
1 packet brown onion soup powder
1 packet cream of mushroom soup powder
800 ml (3¼ cups) water
500 ml (2 cups) grated Cheddar cheese
2.5 ml (½ tsp) dried origanum

Preheat the oven to 180 °C. Heat the oil in a large, flat-bottomed pan. Brown the mince, add the onions and cook until softened. Add the tomato and salt and pepper to taste. Remove from the heat and allow to cool. Transfer to an ovenproof dish and press down firmly. Spread a thin layer of chutney over the meat. Sprinkle the uncooked rice over the meat and cover with the mushrooms and brinjal, pattypan, and baby marrow slices. Mix the soup powders with the water and carefully pour this over the mixture in the dish. Cover with grated cheese and sprinkle with origanum. Cover with foil and bake for 1–1½ hours. Serve hot. **SERVES 8–10**

Note: Remove the foil only when the dish is brought to the table, as its aromas are mouthwatering. This is a versatile dish and any vegetables in season can be included as a variation.

Venison

'Shooting for the pot' became a million-dollar industry

Venison, the prime food of the San, soon became a favourite of the settlers. As they moved into the hinterland the pioneers 'shot for the pot', but this quickly developed into a sport and some animals were hunted almost to extinction. Photographs in the Graaff-Reinet Museum prove hunting was popular. Over the years, hunting and game farming in the Karoo have developed into a multimillion-dollar industry. Low in kilojoules and cholesterol, and virtually free of fat, venison's excellent flavour is highly rated by the health conscious. Long gone are the days when it was marinated in vinegar, red wine and garlic and had what some called a 'wild taste'. Today light marinades, buttermilk and sour cream bring out the delicious, delicate flavour. In the days of the pioneers game was everywhere, springbok migrated in their millions, trampling each other to death and leaving a trail of destruction and hundreds of people preparing biltong. There was no other way to preserve the meat. Augusta de Mist, who travelled into the interior with her father, Commissioner de Mist, tells of a colonist who 'bagged' 17 antelope, each weighing seven or eight hundred pounds. 'The game was disembowelled on the spot, salted, placed in pickling vats and loaded onto the large wagons that accompanied the hunters.' In the 1880s, a Beaufort West tinsmith, C J Heine, went out to 'bag a buck' and his lack of success almost cost him his life. Called out to fix a pump on an isolated farm, he took along his rifle hoping to find some game on the trip back. His luck was out. The buck were within range, but his rifle misfired three times. In disgust, he flung the rifle in the back of his wagon. As he bumped along the rough, virtually non-existent track a shot rang out, but not a soul was in sight. Then, to his horror, he saw blood pouring down his thigh and he realized his own gun had shot him in the buttocks. He struggled on, weak from loss of blood, and at last made it to the doctor's house. He lived to tell his tale, albeit red-faced.

VENISON STEW

1.5 kg kudu or any other venison, cubed
250 ml (1 cup) water
250 ml (1 cup) red wine
250 ml (1 cup) port

MARINADE
250 ml (1 cup) vinegar
250 ml (1 cup) lemon juice
4 whole cloves
2 bay leaves
Salt and freshly ground black pepper to taste

4 onions, roughly chopped
Butter for frying
1 x 820 g can pineapple pieces
500 g (2 punnets) whole button mushrooms
1 packet beef or brown onion soup powder
1 packet mushroom soup powder
1 x 380 g can evaporated milk
250 ml (1 cup) fruit chutney
125 ml (½ cup) Worcestershire sauce

Marinade: Mix all the marinade ingredients together and marinate the meat in this mixture for at least 1–3 days. Pour off the marinade. Mix together the water, red wine and port and cook the meat slowly for 2½–3 hours until tender. Pour off this cooking liquid.

Stew: Brown the onions in a little butter. Add the pineapple pieces with their liquid. Add the mushrooms. Mix the soup powders well with the evaporated milk and add this to the mixture. Add the chutney and Worcestershire sauce and bring the mixture to the boil. Add the cooked meat and cook through for about 15 minutes. Serve with samp or rice. **SERVES 6–8**

Venison Stew

Springbok Fillet with Cranberry Sauce

ᛋPRINGBOK FILLET WITH CRANBERRY OR MUSHROOM AND BLUE CHEESE SAUCE

1 kg springbok fillet
Olive oil
Salt and freshly ground black pepper to taste
5 ml (1 tsp) ground cumin
5 ml (1 tsp) ground coriander
5 ml (1 tsp) mustard powder
2.5 ml (½ tsp) mustard seeds

CRANBERRY SAUCE

1 x 265 g bottle cranberry jelly
Juice of 2 oranges, plus the grated peel of 1 orange
125 ml (½ cup) red wine
5 ml (1 tsp) mustard powder
5 ml (1 tsp) mustard seeds
5 ml (1 tsp) gravy powder
Salt and freshly ground black pepper to taste

MUSHROOM AND BLUE CHEESE SAUCE

Olive oil for frying
250 g (1 punnet) brown mushrooms, wiped clean and chopped
250 ml (1 cup) cream
160 ml (⅔ cup) sherry or brandy
Salt and freshly ground black pepper to taste
100 g blue cheese, crumbled
5 ml (1 tsp) gravy powder
5 ml (1 tsp) cornflour

Clean the fillet and rub well with olive oil. Combine the salt, pepper, cumin, coriander, mustard powder and mustard seeds in a bowl. Mix well and rub this mixture onto the fillet. Set aside. Heat a griddle pan until the smoke rises. Sear the fillet on both sides. Set aside for a while, and then cut into thin slices and grill again just before serving with a cranberry or mushroom and blue cheese sauce (below).

Cranberry sauce: Place the cranberry jelly, orange juice and peel, red wine, mustard powder and mustard seeds in a saucepan and bring to the boil. Cook for a few minutes. Thicken with gravy powder and season to taste.

Mushroom and cheese sauce: Heat a little olive oil in a pan and fry the mushrooms. Add the cream, sherry or brandy, seasoning and cheese and bring to the boil. Mix the gravy powder and cornflour together with a little water and use this to thicken the sauce. SERVES 4–6

The Richmond Supper Club, an elegant new social centre in the village.

SPRINGBOK RIB ROLL

1–1.5 kg springbok rib
50 ml (just over 3 Tbsp) vinegar
Salt to taste
25 ml (5 tsp) Worcestershire sauce
Pinch of ground cloves

FILLING
125 ml (½ cup) sherry
125 ml (½ cup) water
10 ml (2 tsp) lemon juice or vinegar
500 ml (2 cups) mixed dried fruit, chopped
10 ml (2 tsp) sugar
20 ml (4 tsp) Worcestershire sauce
250 ml (1 cup) fresh breadcrumbs
600 g beef or mutton mince
10 ml (2 tsp) butter
20 ml (4 tsp) finely chopped onion
10 ml (2 tsp) chopped fresh parsley
250 g (1 packet) bacon (do not use lean bacon because venison tends to be dry)

The day before: De-bone the springbok rib and sprinkle with the vinegar, salt, Worcestershire sauce and ground cloves. Rub well into the meat and leave to stand overnight.

Bring the sherry, water and lemon juice or vinegar to the boil and poach the dried fruit in this mixture for about 5 minutes. Add the sugar. Stir in Worcestershire sauce. Leave this mixture to stand overnight.

Next day: Preheat the oven to 180 °C. Stir the breadcrumbs and mince into the fruit mix. Melt the butter in a saucepan and sauté the onion and parsley and add to the mixture. Mix well. Cover the meat with rashers of bacon, then place the stuffing on top of this. Roll up and tie securely. Roast in the oven for about 45 minutes, or until the meat is tender. **SERVES 8–10**

WILDSWORS (VENISON SAUSAGE)

50 ml (just over 3 Tbsp) ground coriander
25 ml (5 tsp) whole coriander
10 ml (2 tsp) whole cloves
10 ml (2 tsp) peppercorns
2.5 ml (½ tsp) saltpetre
5 ml (1 tsp) grated nutmeg
12.5 ml (2½ tsp) salt
2.25 kg venison, cut into pieces
500 g raw fat, cut into pieces
250 ml (1 cup) vinegar
150 ml (just under ⅔ cup) Worcestershire sauce

Grind the spices using a pestle and mortar or grinder. Sprinkle the dry ingredients over the meat and fat. Pour over vinegar and Worcestershire sauce. Pass everything through a mincer and stuff the minced mixture into sausage skins.

To cook: Twist off serving-sized pieces – do not cut as the sausage will cook out of its casing – and grill for 10–15 minutes in a hot pan or over the coals until browned and cooked through. **MAKES 2.75 KG**

ℰASY VENISON CASSEROLE

125 g butter
1.4 kg venison, cut into cubes
Salt and freshly ground black pepper to taste
900 g whole small (pickling) onions
125 ml (½ cup) red wine
1 x 115 g can tomato paste
30 ml (2 Tbsp) vinegar
15 ml (1 Tbsp) brown sugar
1 clove garlic, finely chopped
2.5 ml (½ tsp) ground cumin
1 bay leaf
1 cinnamon stick
5 ml (1 tsp) whole cloves
30 ml (2 Tbsp) currants

Melt the butter in a large saucepan. Add the meat and fry lightly, but do not brown. Add all the other ingredients and bring to the boil. Simmer gently for 3 hours (or transfer to a casserole dish and bake at 180 °C for 3 hours) until the meat is tender. Do not stir. Before serving, adjust seasoning. **SERVES 6–8**

A typical grass-thatched worker's cottage nestles on a rise of lush veld in the Klein Karoo.

Blindevinke

BLINDEVINKE (VENISON STEAK WITH BACON)

Kudu or any other big game steak, cut into
6 or 8 portions
Salt and freshly ground black pepper to taste
Herbal spice (Aromat) and barbecue spice
to taste
250 g (1 packet) rindless bacon
Lemon juice for sprinkling
125 ml (½ cup) sheep or pork fat or butter or
olive oil for frying
250 ml (1 cup) fresh cream
5 black peppercorns
1 large bay leaf

Pound each portion of steak lightly on both sides and sprinkle with salt, pepper, herbal and barbecue spice. Place a rasher of bacon on each piece of steak and roll up. Secure with a toothpick and sprinkle with lemon juice. Heat the fat, butter or oil in a heavy-bottomed pan and fry the meat rolls until cooked and nicely browned. Pour over the cream, add the peppercorns and bay leaf and simmer for 10–20 minutes. Serve with rice or baked potatoes. **SERVES 6–8**

BRAISED VENISON WITH SOUR CREAM

Butter, olive oil, margarine or vegetable fat
for frying
250 g (1 punnet) button or brown mushrooms,
wiped clean and sliced
1 x saddle or leg of venison, cut into 1-cm-
thick slices or cubes
2 onions, chopped
1 clove garlic, finely chopped
2.5 ml (½ tsp) caraway seeds
125 ml (½ cup) dry red wine
30 ml (2 Tbsp) lemon juice
30 ml (2 Tbsp) Worcestershire sauce
Salt and freshly ground black pepper to taste
200 ml (just over ¾ cup) sour cream
Chopped fresh parsley for garnishing

Heat the butter, oil or fat in a large saucepan and lightly fry the mushrooms. Remove from the pan and set aside. Fry the venison in the same pan until lightly browned on both sides. Add the onions and garlic. Continue frying until the onions have softened. Add caraway seeds. Pour over the wine, lemon juice and Worcestershire sauce and simmer gently for 1½–2 hours until the meat is tender. Add a little water if necessary. Adjust seasoning. Add the mushrooms and sour cream and heat through, but do not boil again as the mixture will curdle. Garnish with chopped parsley. **SERVES 6–8**

Kudu

Buffon, who described a 'kind of large wild goat with distinctive horns', gave the first account of kudu in the Cape in 1764. Many tried to see this 'noble and lordly kudu', as Bryden called them, and Paravincini di Capelli especially took the route from Beaufort West to Murraysburg because he heard 'this beautiful antelope was to be found there'. However, he only saw some in 1803 in the foothills of the Swartberg, near the Dwyka River towards Laingsburg, and 'they were out of range'. By the mid-1800s kudu seem to have been 'driven back towards the Orange by the ruthless hand of man'. Gordon Cumming, who travelled extensively in the hinterland in the mid-1800s, makes little mention of them.

WARTHOG OR SPRINGBOK WITH PINEAPPLE

1 x 1–1.5 kg shoulder of warthog
(or springbok, or any other small buck)
Salt and freshly ground black pepper to taste
250 ml (1 cup) cake flour
Butter or oil for frying
1 large onion, sliced into rings
1 x 480 g can pineapple pieces, drained
(reserve the liquid)
25 ml (5 tsp) vinegar
25 ml (5 tsp) sugar
2.5 ml (½ tsp) ground ginger
1 x 215 g can tomato purée
Cornflour mixed with a little water
for thickening

Preheat the oven to 160 °C. Season the meat and roll it in the flour, then shake off the excess. Heat the butter or oil in a pan and brown the meat for about 10 minutes. Add the onion and continue frying for a further 5 minutes. Transfer to a casserole dish with the pineapple pieces. Make a sauce from the reserved pineapple juice, vinegar, sugar, ginger and tomato purée by adding these to the pan in which the meat and onions were browned. Bring this mixture to the boil and thicken with cornflour. Cook until the sauce bubbles, and then pour it over the meat in the casserole. Cover and bake in the oven for 1–1½ hours, or until the meat is tender. **SERVES 4–6**

Warthogs

Early writers seldom seem to mention warthogs. However, according to C J Skead's Historical Incidence of Mammals in the Cape Province, *many who wrote of spotting bush and wild pigs had probably seen warthogs. These animals were spotted in the Ceres, Clanwilliam, Upper Karoo and Beaufort West districts and Heinrich Lichtenstein mentions seeing three wild warthog boars at Waaifontein, 24 km north-east of Nelspoort, in 1803. He also mentions seeing quite a few closer to Beaufort West, where 'with lions, they had come out in quest of water'.*

VENISON HEART WITH SWEET SAUCE

1 kudu or gemsbok heart or 4 springbok
hearts
5 ml (1 tsp) salt
Freshly ground black pepper to taste
5 ml (1 tsp) barbecue spice
4 whole cloves
8 whole allspice/pimento berries

SAUCE FOR VENISON HEART
190 ml (¾ cup) seedless raisins
60 ml (¼ cup) sweet sherry or hanepoot wine
375 ml (1½ cups) fresh cream

Preheat the oven to 200 °C. Wash the heart thoroughly to remove the blood from all chambers. Cut off the hard portion at the end and rub the heart inside and out with salt, pepper and barbecue spice. Place the heart on a piece of tin foil large enough to enclose it completely. Add the other spices and close the foil, making sure that it is well sealed. Place on a baking sheet on the middle shelf of the oven and bake for 1½–2 hours, or until tender. Remove from the foil and cut into thin slices. Serve hot or cold with sweet sauce (below).

Sauce: Mince or liquidise the raisins. Mix with the other ingredients and heat the mixture very slowly over a moderate heat until well blended. Take care not to let it burn. Serve this sauce, either hot or cold, with the venison heart. **SERVES 4–6**

Gemsbok

The vast inland plains, says C J Skead, may well have been a stronghold of the gemsbok before man interfered. John Barrow described them as beautiful and dangerous: 'This animal has no timidity. If wounded and pursued it will coolly sit down on its haunches and keep both man and dogs at bay with its long sharp pointed horns.' Barrow reports their numbers were already diminishing east of the Bokkeveld mountains in the Calvinia district in 1799, but this may have been based on hearsay. In 1812 W J Burchell 'came upon a herd' near De Aar. Later he saw some in the Richmond and Hanover districts. In 1831 Steedman found some near Victoria West and later saw some more at the Brak River near Britstown. George Thomson came across San with a carcass near Beaufort West. As a tribute to the gemsbok's courage Lichtenstein, who also saw some near Beaufort West, describes finding skeletons of a leopard and a gemsbok locked together after a fight to the death.

The world famous "red hills" of the Oudtshoorn Calitsdorp area are part of the Buffelskloof Formation, made up of iron-stained conglomerates of Early Cretaceous age, and date back 120 million years.

VENISON LIVER OR KIDNEYS IN SOUR SAUCE

1 springbok liver or 4 kidneys, cleaned
Milk for soaking
Oil for frying
1 onion, chopped
500 ml (2 cups) fresh cream
25 ml (5 tsp) cornflour
375 ml (1½ cups) vinegar
5 ml (1 tsp) salt
Freshly ground black pepper to taste

Cut the liver or kidneys into cubes. Place in a bowl and cover with milk. Leave to soak in order to extract impurities. Drain and dry with paper towel. Heat the oil in a pan and fry the meat until no longer bloody. Add the onion and continue frying until soft. Add a little water if necessary. Cover the saucepan and allow this mixture to simmer for 10–15 minutes, until the meat is well cooked. Mix the cream, cornflour and vinegar together and stir slowly into the cooked meat mixture. Season to taste. Serve on toast or *stywe pap* (stiff mealie meal porridge). **SERVES 4–6**

A typical Karoo farmhouse with its welcoming 'stoep' in Jakkalsfontein, on the road to Merweville.

VENISON TONGUE WITH MUSHROOM SAUCE

1 kudu, gemsbok or eland tongue or
5–6 springbok tongues
1 onion, chopped
5 ml (1 tsp) salt

MUSHROOM SAUCE
20 ml (4 tsp) butter or oil for frying
1 onion, finely chopped
250 g (1 punnet) brown or button mushrooms,
wiped clean and finely sliced
5 ml (1 tsp) dried thyme
10 ml (2 tsp) chopped fresh parsley
30 ml (2 Tbsp) sherry
250 ml (1 cup) reserved cooking liquid
Cornflour for thickening

Wash the tongue thoroughly and place in a heavy-bottomed saucepan with the onion and salt. Cover with cold water. Bring to the boil and cook for 2–3 hours until the meat is soft. Reserve 250 ml (1 cup) of the cooking liquid for the sauce. Peel the tongue while still warm, cut it into slices and place these in an ovenproof dish. Keep warm in the oven preheated to 150 °C while making the sauce (below).

Note: If springbok tongues are used, boil and skin them, but leave them whole.

Mushroom sacue: Heat the butter or oil in a pan and fry the onion until translucent. Add the mushrooms, thyme and parsley and stir-fry for 10 minutes. Add the sherry and cooking liquid. Thicken with cornflour and pour the sauce over the tongue. Return to the oven for 10–15 minutes before serving.
SERVES 4–6

The Magic of the Eland

The Dutch named the eland because it reminded them of an elk. On the scorched plains of the Karoo the eland – the biggest, most powerful, yet gentlest and most civilised of antelopes according to Sir Laurens van der Post – produces a special music and magic. In A Mantis Carol, he writes: 'The mantis (the god of the San) loves to sit between the toes of the black, patent-leather foot of the eland. This buck's foot expands and the toes part as it steps on the desert sand. This prevents the eland from sinking in too deeply. As the majestic antelope lifts its foot, the toes snap together with a sharp, electric click. Often, lying in the shade of a thorn tree, I listened to the sounds of a herd of eland grazing. The delicate and precise magnetic click made magic music for me.' Sir Laurens said in time he was able to understand, not rationally, but emotionally, why a god would take its position where this kind of electricity issued. Archaeologists say the eland was as important to the San as the lamb is to Christians. One only has to look at their rock art to appreciate its special, almost mystical stature. The San are said to have had a 'special' note in their voices when speaking of eland. The eland song was one of their most evocative, said Sir Laurens. 'It overflowed with nostalgia for the source from where life itself had come.'

KUDU PIE IN COLD WATER PASTRY

1 kg kudu meat, cut into pieces (more if the
meat includes a lot of bones)
30 ml (2 Tbsp) cake flour
30 ml (2 Tbsp) ground coriander
2.5 ml (½ tsp) ground cloves
10 ml (2 tsp) salt
250 ml (1 cup) apricot chutney
Garlic and herb seasoning to taste

COLD WATER PASTRY
750 ml (3 cups) cake flour
4 ml (¾ tsp) salt
250 g frozen butter
1 egg
100–150 ml ice-cold water
5 ml (1 tsp) cream of tartar

Boil the meat until it is tender and falls from the bones. Cool and remove all the bones. Cut the meat into smaller pieces (if necessary). Place all the other ingredients in a saucepan, bring to the boil and then pour over the meat. Mix to ensure everything is well blended. Place in a pie dish, cover with cold water pastry (below) and bake in a preheated oven at 180 °C for 20 minutes until the pie crust is golden brown.

Note: This is an ideal way of using the excess little bits and pieces, as well as trimmings, offcuts and bones from larger cuts when meat is being prepared for the freezer during hunting season. Most cooks also prepare a large pot of fynvleis (fine meat) for stews and brawns at this time.

Pastry: Sift the flour and salt together into a large bowl. Grate 125 g butter into the flour (return the rest to the freezer). Rub the butter lightly into the flour using fingertips. Make a hollow in this mixture. Beat the egg and add. Add iced water in small amounts, stirring all the time until a dough is formed. Knead this dough until it becomes elastic and no longer sticks to your fingers. Place in the refrigerator for 5 minutes to rest. Then, roll out to 50 cm x 30 cm x 1 cm thick, sprinkle with cream of tartar and grate the rest of the butter over the pastry. Fold the pastry in half and roll out until small bubbles appear. Fold up and rest in the refrigerator for one day before using. **SERVES 4–6**

SPRINGBOK FYNVLEIS PIE

1.5 kg meaty loin, neck and shin bones
2 onions, chopped
7 whole cloves
½ nutmeg, grated
125 ml (½ cup) brown vinegar (more can be
added if desired)
125 ml (½ cup) apricot chutney
1 packet cream of chicken soup powder mixed
with 15 ml (1 Tbsp) cake flour
Salt and freshly ground black pepper to taste

QUICK PASTRY TOPPING
1 egg, beaten
125 ml (½ cup) oil
125 ml (½ cup) milk
250 ml (1 cup) self-raising flour
Salt

Place the meat (including the bones), onions, cloves, nutmeg, vinegar and chutney into a large saucepan, cover with water and bring to the boil. Cook until the meat easily falls from the bones. Check and add liquid if necessary because venison cooked down to fynvleis easily becomes 'dry'. Stir to loosen the meat, and then remove the bones. Bind the cooking liquid with the chicken soup/flour mixture, cook through and scoop into a pie dish. Cover with Quick Pastry (below) and bake at 180 °C for 30 minutes until the pie crust is golden brown.

Pastry topping: Beat the egg, oil and milk together well. Add the flour and salt and mix well. Scoop spoonfuls onto the top of the cooked meat. (Once in the oven it will settle over the top of the pie on its own.) **SERVES 6–8**

Kudu Pie in Cold Water Pastry

Storm clouds gather to bring welcome rain to the parched Karoo landscape.

Poultry, Ostrich and Game Birds

Poultry

Excellent for family feasts or entertaining

Poultry has always been a reliable stand-by for anything from quiet suppers to elegant entertaining. Many early writers describe menus featuring roast chicken with fulsome stuffings and flavoursome accompaniments. Epicurean and writer C Louis Leipoldt maintained that the earliest of settlers in places like the Karoo would have feasted on 'barnyard fowl, mostly superfluous cockerels, ducks and ducklings, among which the muscovy was reckoned the choicest, as well as geese and pigeons'. Old chickens went into the soup pot or were boiled with vegetables and herbs to make a wholesome pie. Poultry seemed best when pot-roasted with 'a bunch of herbs, a blade of mace, peppercorns, onions and a dash of wine to add to its savour,' he said. Leipoldt's recipe for 'really tasty stewed fowl' uses all these ingredients and he recommended thickening the gravy with an egg yolk and a tablespoon of tamarind water (or lemon juice). 'Stir this into the gravy, and let it thicken, but do not boil; pour it over the fowl and serve.' Hinterland cooks used delicious stuffings to 'extend the fowl', and they often added 'a bit of pork fat' for a richer flavour. Cold chicken was central to every *platteland* (country) picnic and an essential part of *padkos* (food for eating on a journey). Many Beaufort Westers have memories of stops in Meiringspoort and wades in the river, followed by cold chicken drumsticks, buttered home-made bread and hot coffee from a flask.

CHICKEN THIGHS WITH LEEKS AND MUSHROOMS

30 ml (2 Tbsp) olive oil
1.5 kg chicken thighs
Cake flour for dusting
1 onion, finely chopped
1 clove garlic, finely chopped
3 leeks, well washed and sliced into rings
4 sticks celery, finely sliced
4 large black mushrooms, wiped and sliced
4 whole cloves
1 bay leaf
5 ml (1 tsp) chicken spice
5 ml (1 tsp) chopped fresh thyme or 2.5 ml (½ tsp) dried thyme (optional)
425 ml (1¾ cups) warm chicken stock
125 ml (½ cup) sour cream
50 ml (just over 3 Tbsp) chopped fresh parsley
Salt and freshly ground black pepper to taste

THICK WHITE SAUCE
¼ onion
6 peppercorns
250 ml (1 cup) milk
40 g butter
40 ml (just under 3 Tbsp) flour
Salt to taste

Heat the olive oil in a saucepan. Dust the chicken pieces with flour and shake off excess. Brown on both sides. Remove and set aside. Add the onion, garlic, leeks, celery and mushrooms to the pan and fry for 5–10 minutes. Return the chicken to the pan. Add the cloves, bay leaf, spice, thyme and chicken stock. Cover and simmer over a low heat until the chicken is tender – about 45 minutes. In the meantime prepare the white sauce.

White sauce: Add the onion and the peppercorns to the milk and simmer for 4–7 minutes. Cool and strain. Melt the butter and add the flour. Stir continuously and cook for 2 minutes. Add the strained milk. Simmer until the sauce thickens, stirring continuously. Cook for about 5 minutes. Season. Remove the bay leaf and cloves from the chicken mixture. Stir in the white sauce and simmer for a further 5 minutes. Stir in the sour cream and parsley. Check seasoning. Stir and serve immediately. **SERVES 6–8**

Chicken Thighs with Leeks and Mushrooms

$\mathcal{T}$ASTY CHICKEN STEW

10 chicken thighs
2 x 425 g cans cream of chicken soup
1.5 litres (6 cups) water
500 ml (2 cups) chopped celery
4 onions, quartered
10 ml (2 tsp) salt
5 ml (1 tsp) chicken seasoning
Freshly ground black pepper
8 potatoes, peeled and quartered
6 carrots, sliced
500 g (½ packet) frozen peas
Cornflour for thickening

Combine the chicken pieces, soup, water, celery, onions, salt and seasonings in a large flat-bottomed pot and cook over a low heat for 45–60 minutes. Check the liquid from time to time. Add the potatoes and carrots and cook for another 30 minutes, continuing to check that the stew does not become dry. Add the peas and simmer for a few minutes until the peas are cooked. Skim off any fat, and thicken with cornflour, if necessary. Serve on a bed of rice. **SERVES 8–10**

Spandaukop towers over Graaff-Reinet, the third oldest town in South Africa and virtually a living museum.

MINI CHICKEN PIES

PASTRY
500 ml (2 cups) cake flour
15 ml (1 Tbsp) baking powder
5 ml (1 tsp) salt
250 g butter
2 eggs
5 ml (1 tsp) vinegar or lemon juice

FILLING
1 x 425 g can cream of chicken soup
250 ml (1 cup) milk
5 ml (1 tsp) salt
25 ml (5 tsp) butter
25 ml (5 tsp) cornflour
2 eggs, beaten
250 ml (1 cup) grated Cheddar cheese
500 ml (2 cups) chopped cooked chicken
Pinch of cayenne pepper

Pastry: Sift the dry ingredients into a bowl. Rub in the butter. Beat the eggs and vinegar together and mix into the dry ingredients to form a dough. Refrigerate for 30 minutes.

Filling: Preheat the oven to 180 °C. Mix the soup with milk, salt and butter. Boil until cooked and thicken with cornflour. Add the eggs and beat well to ensure that the eggs do not curdle. Cool, and then add the cheese, cooked chicken and cayenne pepper. Roll out the pastry to about 3 mm thick and (using a saucer as a guide) cut into circles to fit into the 'holes' of a muffin pan. Place the pastry circles into greased muffin pans. Spoon the chicken mixture into each and top with grated cheese. Bake in the oven for 25–30 minutes until the pastry is cooked and the cheese topping is golden brown. **MAKES 12**

EASY CHICKEN PIE WITH 'SOFT' PASTRY

Boil a good-sized chicken with an onion and your favourite herbs and spices. When done, cool and remove the skin and bones. Flake the meat, or chop into smaller pieces, and place in an ovenproof dish with sufficient juice to ensure a succulent pie.

PASTRY
60 ml (4 Tbsp) cake flour
5 ml (1 tsp) baking powder
2.5 ml (½ tsp) salt
Freshly grated nutmeg
60 ml (4 Tbsp) butter
1 egg, beaten
A little milk to make the mixture into a dough

Preheat the oven to 180 °C. Sift the flour, baking powder and salt together. Add the nutmeg. Rub in the butter and mix into a soft dough with beaten egg and a little milk. Place small spoonfuls of this soft dough over the top of flaked chicken mixture. Place in the oven and bake for about 30 minutes until the pastry is golden brown. **SERVES 6–8**

SAVOURY CHICKEN PIE

PASTRY

125 g soft butter

1 egg, beaten

12.5 ml (2½ tsp) buttermilk

350 ml (just under 1½ cups) self-raising flour

5 ml (1 tsp) salt

2.5 ml (½ tsp) cayenne pepper

125 ml (½ cup) grated Cheddar cheese

CREAMY CHICKEN FILLING

8 chicken thighs

10 ml (2 tsp) tomato sauce

½ packet (30 g) cream of mushroom soup powder

½ packet (30 g) onion soup powder

10 ml (2 tsp) chutney

250 ml (1 cup) water

125 ml (½ cup) mayonnaise

125 ml (½ cup) grated Cheddar cheese

CHICKEN AND BLUE CHEESE FILLING

8 chicken pieces, cooked and de-boned

Salt and freshly ground black pepper to taste

15 ml (1 Tbsp) butter

1 medium onion, finely chopped or grated

2 baby marrows (courgettes), finely chopped or grated

60 ml (¼ cup) crumbled blue cheese

60 ml (¼ cup) grated Cheddar cheese

1 egg, beaten

60 ml (¼ cup) milk

Pastry: Place the butter, egg and buttermilk in bowl and mix well. Add the flour and seasonings and mix well. Add the cheese. Roll out the dough on a lightly floured surface to about 3 mm thick and line a 23 cm pie plate.

Creamy chicken filling: Season the chicken pieces and boil them in a little water until tender – 20–25 minutes. Cool slightly and de-bone, but leave the meat in the saucepan. Preheat the oven to 180 °C. Mix the rest of the filling ingredients together, except the cheese, and add to the chicken. Simmer for a few minutes, and then cool. Place this filling into the unbaked pie shell, sprinkle with cheese and bake for 50–60 minutes until set. Serve hot. **SERVES 6**

Chicken and blue cheese filling: Place the chicken pieces in a saucepan, season and boil with a little water until tender – 20–25 minutes. Cool the chicken and de-bone. Preheat the oven to 180 °C. Heat the butter in a pan and sauté the onion and baby marrows. Add to the chicken. Add the blue cheese and adjust the seasoning. Spoon the filling into the unbaked pie shells and cover with Cheddar cheese. Mix the egg and milk together and pour this over. Bake for 50–60 minutes until set. **SERVES 6**

RED CHICKEN

1 red onion, finely chopped

2 kg chicken pieces

90 ml (6 Tbsp) tomato sauce

30 ml (2 Tbsp) chutney

45 ml (3 Tbsp) Worcestershire sauce

125 ml (½ cup) red wine

100 ml (a bit under ½ cup) black Rooibos tea

15 ml (1 Tbsp) lime juice (optional)

5 ml (1 tsp) mustard powder

Salt and freshly ground black pepper to taste

Preheat the oven to 180 °C. Place a layer of red onion on the bottom of a casserole dish and then place the chicken pieces on top of this. Mix all the other ingredients and pour over the chicken. Cover and bake in the oven for about 1 hour. Remove the lid and cook for a further 15–20 minutes until the chicken is tender and the sauce has thickened. If necessary, thicken with cornflour. **SERVES 6–8**

Savoury Chicken Pie with Blue Cheese Filling

Roast Duck with Nut Stuffing and Quince Jelly Sauce

ROAST DUCK WITH NUT STUFFING AND QUINCE JELLY SAUCE

1.3 kg duck
45 ml (3 Tbsp) brown sugar
15 ml (1 Tbsp) salt
300 ml (1¼ cups) warm water

STUFFING
15 ml (1 Tbsp) butter or oil for frying
1 large onion, finely chopped
1 clove garlic, crushed
100–125 g button mushrooms, wiped and finely chopped
15 ml (1 Tbsp) finely chopped fresh sage or 5 ml (1 tsp) dried sage
15 ml (1 Tbsp) finely chopped fresh parsley
50 g (½ cup) walnuts, finely chopped
60 ml (¼ cup) finely chopped cashew nuts
60 ml (¼ cup) finely chopped Brazil nuts
160 ml (⅔ cup) fresh white breadcrumbs
1 egg
Some giblet stock or water to moisten

SAUCE
Reserved giblets and neck
1 onion, sliced
1 carrot, thinly sliced
1 bay leaf
45 ml (3 Tbsp) sweet red wine
45 ml (3 Tbsp) quince jelly
10 ml (2 tsp) lemon juice
Salt and freshly ground black pepper to taste
Cornflour mixed to a paste with a little water for thickening
Thinly sliced lemon peel for garnishing

Clean the duck (reserve the neck and giblets for the stock) and dry thoroughly. Dissolve the sugar and salt in the warm water and soak the duck in this mixture for a few hours. Drain the duck, dry well and stuff.

Stuffing: Preheat the oven to 160 °C. Heat the butter or oil in a pan and fry the onion and garlic until softened. Add the mushrooms and fry for about a minute. Add the herbs and stir-fry lightly. Set aside. Mix the nuts in a large bowl. Add the breadcrumbs, onion mixture, egg and a little giblet stock and mix to form a stiff stuffing. Stuff the duck and sew closed. Prick all over and roast in the oven for 2–2½ hours until tender. When done, remove the duck from the pan, cut it into portions and place in an ovenproof dish. Carefully remove the stuffing from the breast cavity and slice with a sharp knife. Place in a separate dish and keep warm.

Sauce: While the duck is roasting, make a stock from the giblets and neck (do not include the liver) by boiling them with the onion, carrot and bay leaf for about 30 minutes. Strain and set aside (you will need 250 ml (1 cup) for the sauce). Once the duck has finished roasting, skim the fat from the pan and add the stock to the pan juices. Stir well. Add the wine, quince jelly, lemon juice, salt and pepper. Simmer gently for a few minutes to allow the flavours to develop. Thicken with cornflour and pour over the duck. Return to the oven to reheat for a few minutes before serving. Place the slices of lemon peel into warm water for a while to allow them to curl and use to garnish the duck. **SERVES 6**

Note: If quince jelly is not available, use grape or apple jelly or even grape jam. For a dish with a difference, add 200 ml (just over ¾ cup) seeded fresh grapes to the gravy.

ROAST DUCK WITH PARSNIPS AND RED WINE

1 large duck (1.5 kg), cut into portions
Salt and freshly ground black pepper
100 g (¾ cup) cake flour
12.5 ml (2½ tsp) oil
1 onion, finely chopped
1 bay leaf
5 ml (1 tsp) dried thyme
3 large parsnips, peeled and chopped
3 large carrots, peeled and chopped
250 g (1 punnet) brown mushrooms, wiped
clean and sliced
150 ml (just under ⅔ cup) red wine
Cornflour mixed to a paste for thickening

Preheat the oven to 180 °C. Season the duck portions well and toss in flour. Heat the oil and fry the portions until golden brown. Using a slotted spoon remove the duck and place in a casserole dish. Fry the onion with the bay leaf and thyme until the onion becomes translucent, and then add to the casserole. Place the parsnips, carrots and mushrooms in the pan and stir-fry for 5 minutes. Add to the casserole dish. Add the wine to the pan and stir to deglaze the pan. Pour this over the duck and cover the casserole dish with a tight-fitting lid or tin foil. Place in the oven and cook for 40–45 minutes until the duck portions are tender. Thicken the gravy and serve hot. **SERVES 4–6**

Note: Traditionally, a can of red cherries or orange juice, orange rind and about 30 ml (2 Tbsp) orange marmalade were added to a casserole of duck, but in this recipe the parsnips and carrots give a delightfully different and delicious flavour. Other seasonal vegetables, such as peas, lima beans or broad beans, can be added for colour and to ring the flavour changes. For an exotic version, fry a few slices of pineapple and use these as a garnish.

Goose with Porcupine

Marinate an old, well-plucked goose for a week in the fridge with brandy, oil and any bits of port or sherry that you can sneak out of the liquor cupboard. If you have some witblits (moonshine) to mix with the brandy it will make the dish even more special. Take a quarter porcupine and cut it into chunks. Stew the porcupine and goose very slowly overnight with onions. Serve with potatoes.

Note: This recipe is very rich, but quite delicious! Porcupine was a delicacy of the early Karoo. Augusta, only daughter of Commissioner de Mist, who accompanied him on an official journey into the interior in 1803, was served some after an exhausting day. 'A colonist's wife offered us some broth and porcupine meat she had prepared. It was a small meal, but it gave us strength.' According to Lawrence Green, the skin of the porcupine was considered a rare delicacy. After the spines were removed and the hair singed off, the skin was soaked in brine for 24 hours. It was then boiled in fresh water, cut into strips, braaied (barbecued) over the coals and then served with lemon and butter.

Stark winter trees border a dwindling water supply of a farm dam near Fraserburg.

Home-made Ostrich Burgers

Ostrich

Excellent eating from neck to tail

Ostrich meat is excellent. It cooks quickly and it's frequently touted as a healthy alternative to other meats because it's low in fat, cholesterol and kilojoules, but rich in protein and iron. Fillet and steaks are by far the most popular cuts, but the neck (which is over a metre long) is delicious when stewed or stuffed with minced giblets, dried fruit and fresh herbs. Some have been known to roast an ostrich leg, well larded to prevent it from drying out. Way back in the 1970s, history was made in Cape Town when a whole ostrich was de-boned, stuffed and roasted for an outdoor feast. Believe it or not, the parson's nose – the bird's large tail-end – which is sufficient for one or perhaps two people, is considered a delicacy when gently braaied over the coals or roasted in the oven. Preparation is a titch tedious because each 'nose' needs to be de-glanded and have all its pin feathers carefully tweezed out. However, connoisseurs agree that when well seasoned and sprinkled with herbs this titbit is definitely worth the effort. Ostrich egg omelette or scramble makes for a delicious breakfast, but remember these are the largest eggs in the world and each is equal to 24 hen's eggs. A single egg can weigh up to six kilograms. Legend has it that the San thought of the sun as evil and they believed ostriches sat on their eggs, not to incubate them, but to keep the sun from killing them.

HOME-MADE OSTRICH BURGERS

1 onion, finely chopped
Oil for frying
500 g ostrich mince
1 clove garlic, crushed
15 ml (1 Tbsp) capers, chopped
2 anchovy fillets, chopped
5 ml (1 tsp) Worcestershire sauce
1 slice wholewheat bread, crumbled and soaked in 60 ml (¼ cup) water
1 egg, beaten
Salt and freshly ground black pepper to taste
6 soft hamburger buns
3 tomatoes, sliced
1 onion, sliced
1 lettuce, separated into leaves

Fry the onion in a little oil until translucent. Place the mince, onion, garlic, capers, anchovy, Worcestershire sauce, soaked bread, egg and seasoning in a large bowl and mix well. Knead slightly to ensure the mixture sticks well together and then divide into six. Form into patties. Pan-fry until golden brown and cooked through. Serve immediately on hamburger buns with tomato, onion and lettuce. **MAKES 6**

ℳouthwatering Sauces for Fillets and Steaks

4–6 ostrich fillets or steaks, seasoned on both sides with salt and freshly ground black pepper

Set the steaks aside in the refrigerator for at least 1 hour. Remove from the refrigerator and allow to rest at room temperature for another hour before braaiing or pan-frying. Before placing them on the coals or in the pan, wipe both sides of each steak with paper towel to remove excess moisture. Cook for 3–7 minutes, depending on whether the steaks are to be medium-rare or well done. Remove from the heat and place on a serving dish. Allow to rest – do not cut immediately or all the juices will run out. Before serving, cut the steaks into thin slices and cover with sauce. Reheat, if necessary, or serve cold. **SERVES 4–6**

SPECIAL 'MONKEY GLAND' SAUCE

1 onion, finely chopped
1 clove garlic, crushed
1 bay leaf
Salt and freshly ground black pepper to taste
250 ml (1 cup) water
625 ml (2½ cups) tomato sauce
125 ml (½ cup) vinegar
190 ml (¾ cup) Worcestershire sauce
500 ml (2 cups) soy sauce
Cornflour mixed to a paste with cold water for thickening

Place the onion, garlic, bay leaf, salt and pepper in a saucepan with the water and bring to the boil. Add the rest of the ingredients, except the cornflour, and simmer for about 10 minutes. Remove the bay leaf and thicken the sauce with a little cornflour. This sauce will keep well in the refrigerator for two to three weeks. **MAKES ABOUT 1 LITRE**

KANNALAND HERB SAUCE

60 ml (¼ cup) sunflower oil
60 ml (¼ cup) olive oil
30 ml (2 Tbsp) white wine vinegar
30 ml (2 Tbsp) French mustard
30 ml (2 Tbsp) mayonnaise
60 ml (4 Tbsp) finely chopped fresh parsley
10 ml (2 tsp) finely chopped fresh thyme or
5 ml (1 tsp) dried thyme
10 ml (2 tsp) finely chopped fresh marjoram or
5 ml (1 tsp) dried marjoram

Mix the sunflower and olive oils and the vinegar together and divide between two bowls. Add mustard and mayonnaise to the first bowl and beat briskly with a balloon whisk (don't use an electric mixer – this will curdle the mixture). Pour this mixture onto the bottom of a large serving platter and arrange the meat slices on top. Mix the herbs with the rest of the oil and vinegar mixture and pour over the meat. Garnish with thin shavings of Parmesan cheese. Serve hot with mashed potatoes or cold with a green salad and a variety of fresh, home-made breads. **MAKES ABOUT 200 ML**

GREEN PEPPERCORN AND BRANDY SAUCE

500 ml (2 cups) fresh cream
45 ml (3 Tbsp) preserved green peppercorns, rinsed in cold water
125 ml (½ cup) brandy
250 ml (1 cup) beef stock
Salt and freshly ground black pepper to taste

Pour the cream into a saucepan and add the peppercorns. Bring to the boil over medium heat, stirring continuously to ensure that the mixture does not boil over. Simmer for 10 minutes to allow the flavours to develop and the sauce to reduce. The sauce should then be thick enough to coat the back of a spoon. Add the brandy and beef stock and continue cooking until the sauce thickens. Add salt and pepper to taste. Remove from the heat and keep warm until serving. **MAKES ABOUT 750 ML**

Ostrich Fillet with Kannaland Herb Sauce

$\mathcal{S}$HEPHERD'S PIE

30 ml (2 Tbsp) butter
1 kg ostrich mince
1 carrot, peeled and grated
30–60 ml (2–4 Tbsp) tomato purée
30 ml (2 Tbsp) tomato sauce
90 ml (6 Tbsp) red wine
5 ml (1 tsp) chilli flakes
2 cloves garlic, chopped
10 ml (2 tsp) ground cumin
50 ml (just over 3 Tbsp) chutney
Spring onions to taste (optional)
Salt and freshly ground black pepper to taste

TOPPING
6 potatoes, peeled and cubed
4 heads broccoli, cut into florets
60 ml (4 Tbsp) butter
Salt and freshly ground black pepper to taste
Fresh parsley for garnishing

Preheat the oven to 180 °C. Heat the butter in a saucepan until it foams; add the mince and sauté for 6–8 minutes until brown. Add the carrot, tomato purée and sauce, red wine and chilli flakes. Stir well. Increase the heat and cook quickly for 2–4 minutes. Add the garlic, cumin, chutney and spring onions if using. Season to taste. Simmer for 5 minutes before scooping into a suitable ovenproof dish.

Topping: Boil the potatoes for 6–8 minutes, add the broccoli pieces and cook for a further 4–6 minutes, or until both are tender. Drain and mash well. Stir in the butter and seasoning. Scoop over the top of the meat mixture and bake on the centre shelf of the oven for 20–25 minutes, or until done. Serve hot garnished with parsley. **SERVES 6–8**

The Lord Milner Hotel, Matjiesfontein.

SPICY OSTRICH MEATBALLS

1 kg ostrich mince
1 onion, finely chopped
2 cloves garlic, finely chopped
15 ml (1 Tbsp) finely chopped fresh parsley
15 ml (1 Tbsp) finely chopped fresh
coriander leaves
2.5 ml (½ tsp) cayenne pepper
2.5 ml (½ tsp) freshly ground black pepper
2.5 ml (½ tsp) ground ginger
2.5 ml (½ tsp) ground cardamom
5 ml (1 tsp) ground cumin
5 ml (1 tsp) paprika

SAUCE
30 ml (2 Tbsp) olive oil
1 onion, finely chopped
2 cloves garlic, finely chopped
10 ml (2 tsp) ground cinnamon
5 ml (1 tsp) paprika
2 x 410 g cans chopped tomatoes
30 ml (2 Tbsp) apricot jam
60 ml (¼ cup) chopped fresh coriander leaves

Meatballs: Preheat the oven to 180 °C. Grease two baking sheets. Place all the ingredients for the meatballs into a bowl and mix well. Season with salt and pepper. Roll into balls and place these on the baking sheets. Bake for 15–20 minutes until nicely browned.

Sauce: Heat the oil in a large pan. Add the onion and cook over medium heat for 5 minutes until softened. Add the garlic and spices and cook for a few more minutes to allow the flavours to develop. Stir in the tomatoes and apricot jam and bring to the boil. Reduce the heat and simmer for 20 minutes. Add the cooked meatballs and simmer for a further 10 minutes until they are well cooked and the sauce has thickened. Stir in the coriander, adjust seasoning and serve hot over spaghetti. **SERVES 4–6**

OSTRICH CURRY

30 ml (2 Tbsp) oil
2 onions, finely chopped
2 cloves garlic, crushed
2 green chillies, de-seeded and finely chopped
1 x 5 cm piece fresh ginger, peeled and grated
7.5 ml (1½ tsp) turmeric
10 ml (2 tsp) ground cumin
15 ml (1 Tbsp) ground coriander
2.5–5 ml (½–1 tsp) chilli powder (as preferred)
30 ml (2 Tbsp) water
1 kg ostrich steak, cut into cubes or
goulash strips
5 ml (1 tsp) salt
1 x 410 g can chopped tomatoes
125 ml (½ cup) coconut milk

Heat the oil in a heavy flat-bottomed pan with a close-fitting lid. Fry the onions over medium heat for about 10 minutes until golden brown. Stir constantly to prevent burning. Add the garlic, fresh chillies and ginger and fry for a further 2 minutes. Keep stirring to ensure that the mixture does not burn. Place the turmeric, cumin, coriander and chilli powder in a small bowl, add the water and stir to a paste. Add the mixture to the pan and stir constantly for 2 minutes. Add the meat in small batches and brown well, stirring to ensure that the meat is well coated with the spice mixture. Add the salt and the tomatoes with their liquid. Bring to the boil. Cover. Reduce the heat and simmer for 45–60 minutes. About 30 minutes before the end of the cooking time, stir in the coconut milk. Before serving, adjust seasoning and thicken the sauce if necessary. **SERVES 4–6**

OSTRICH NECK AND ASPARAGUS QUICHE

1 ostrich neck, cut into pieces
1 onion, chopped
5 whole cloves
Salt and freshly ground black pepper to taste

PASTRY
250 ml (1 cup) cake flour
250 ml (1 cup) grated Cheddar cheese
10 ml (2 tsp) grated Parmesan cheese
125 g softened butter
Salt and freshly ground black pepper to taste
Pinch of cayenne pepper
Egg white for brushing

FILLING
1 bunch spring onions, chopped
25 ml (5 tsp) butter
15 ml (1 Tbsp) oil
1 onion, chopped
200 g (¾ packet) bacon, chopped
200 g leeks, well washed and finely sliced
4 slices ham, chopped
500 ml (2 cups) cooked and cubed ostrich neck (see above)
1 x 420 g can asparagus tips
25 ml (5 tsp) tomato sauce
250 ml (1 cup) grated Cheddar cheese
15 ml (1 Tbsp) cake flour
4 eggs, beaten
500 ml (2 cups) fresh cream
Grated nutmeg (optional)
Pinch of cayenne pepper

Place the neck, onion, cloves and seasoning in a saucepan, cover with water and bring to the boil. Reduce the heat and simmer gently for 1½–2 hours until the meat is tender. Remove from the heat, cool and remove the bones. Cut into cubes.

Pastry: Mix all the ingredients well together to form a soft dough. Press the dough into a 20–22 cm springform pan or large ovenproof pie dish, ensuring that it is evenly spread out. Prick the base, brush with egg white and place in the refrigerator to rest while the filling is being prepared.

Filling: Preheat the oven to 180 °C. Sprinkle 50 ml (just over 3 Tbsp) chopped spring onions evenly over the pastry base. Heat the butter and oil in a pan and sauté the onion, bacon and leeks for a few minutes. Add the rest of the spring onions and fry lightly. Remove from the heat. Add the ham and ostrich neck meat. Mix lightly, but thoroughly. Divide the mixture in two. Spread one half over the pastry base. Drain the asparagus tips and spread them evenly over the meat mixture. Spread the rest of the meat mixture over the asparagus. Dot with tomato sauce and top with grated cheese. Beat the flour into the eggs. Add the cream, a pinch of nutmeg if using, and a pinch of cayenne pepper. Mix lightly. Pour over the filling. Bake in the oven for 30–40 minutes, or until the top is light brown and the mixture set. **SERVES 6–8**

Note: If a less rich topping is desired, milk can be used instead of cream and only cooking oil can be used instead of adding butter. The butter, however, does add to the flavour. If preferred, a mixture of half cream/half sour cream or half milk/half cream can be used.

OSTRICH MINCE ROLL IN FLAKY PASTRY

MINCE ROLL
500 g ostrich mince

1 medium onion, chopped

125 g (½ packet) chopped bacon or 250 g mutton mince

30 ml (2 Tbsp) chopped fresh parsley

1 egg

125 ml (½ cup) fresh breadcrumbs

1 ml (¼ tsp) dried origanum

2.5 ml (½ tsp) salt (or to taste)

2.5 ml (½ tsp) freshly ground black pepper

20 ml (4 tsp) mushroom or onion soup powder

1 small apple, peeled, cored and grated

15 ml (1 Tbsp) lemon juice

FILLING
250 ml (1 cup) grated Cheddar cheese

30 ml (2 Tbsp) grated Parmesan cheese

20 ml (4 tsp) butter

15 ml (1 Tbsp) finely chopped onion

1 clove garlic, crushed

125 g (½ packet) bacon, chopped (if using mutton mince for the meat base, increase this to 250 g (1 packet) bacon)

250 g (1 punnet) button mushrooms, wiped clean and chopped

250 g frozen spinach, defrosted and drained

125 ml (½ cup) fresh breadcrumbs

125 ml (½ cup) smooth cream cheese

1 egg

1 ml (¼ tsp) salt

1 ml (¼ tsp) freshly ground black pepper

2.5 ml (½ tsp) cayenne pepper

15–30 ml (1–2 Tbsp) finely chopped fresh parsley

10 ml (2 tsp) lemon juice

1–2.5 ml (¼–½ tsp) grated nutmeg

2.5 ml (½ tsp) dried mixed herbs

30–45 ml (2–3 Tbsp) chopped almonds

PASTRY
1 x 400 g roll flaky pastry

1 egg yolk, beaten

10 ml (2 tsp) milk

Mince roll: Mix all the ingredients well together with a fork and set aside while the filling is being prepared.

Filling: Preheat the oven to 180 °C. Place the meat mixture on a double sheet of foil and press out lightly into a rectangular shape, 35 cm x 25 cm x 1 cm thick. Sprinkle with the Cheddar and Parmesan cheeses. Heat the butter in a saucepan and sauté the onion, garlic, bacon and mushrooms. Set aside to cool and then mix the rest of the ingredients into the bacon and onion mixture. Mix well. Spread evenly over the meat and cheese. Using the foil to assist you, carefully roll up the meat. Leave the roll on the foil so that it does not break, and place it on a baking sheet. Cover with foil to prevent it from drying out. Bake in the oven for about 1 hour, until done. Remove from the oven and allow to cool.

Pastry: Increase the oven temperature to 220 °C. Roll out the pastry. Place the cooked and cooled mince roll on top and fold over to close. If desired, cut leaves or decorations from the pastry trimmings and place these on top. Mix the egg yolk and milk and use this to brush the pastry. Place on a baking sheet and bake for 40–50 minutes until the pastry has risen and is golden brown. **SERVES 10–12**

Donkey carts are a traditional mode of transport in the Karoo.

Game Birds

GUINEA FOWL CASSEROLE

125 g (½ packet) bacon
3 apples, peeled, cored and sliced
3 guinea fowl, breasts and de-boned thighs only
Seasoned flour
Oil for frying
100 g (⅔ cup) raisins, sultanas or pitted prunes
375 ml (1½ cups) chicken stock
375 ml (1½ cups) red wine
30 ml (2 Tbsp) fruit chutney
2 bay leaves
30 ml (2 Tbsp) quince or red currant jelly
60 ml (¼ cup) sour cream (optional)

Preheat the oven to 180 °C. Fry the bacon until crisp, and then set aside. Fry the apple slices in the bacon fat, then set aside. Shake the guinea fowl pieces in a plastic bag filled with seasoned flour, shake off the excess and fry lightly in a little oil. Place the guinea fowl pieces, dried fruit, chicken stock, red wine, chutney and bay leaves in a casserole dish and bake in the oven for 3–4 hours, or until the meat is tender. Add the bacon and apple slices and heat through. Just before serving, stir in the jelly and add the sour cream (it may be necessary to remove some of the sauce). Once the cream has been added, reheat, but do not boil. Serve immediately. **SERVES 6–8**

STUFFED GUINEA FOWL WITH VAN DER HUM SAUCE

2 guinea fowl
6–8 rashers streaky bacon
1 small onion, chopped
1 carrot, sliced
375 ml (1½ cups) chicken stock
Grated peel and juice of 1 orange
60 ml (¼ cup) Van der Hum liqueur

WALNUT STUFFING
45 ml (3 Tbsp) butter
1 onion, finely chopped
2 sticks celery, finely chopped
5 slices bread, crusts removed, crumbled
100 g (1 cup) walnuts, finely chopped
5 ml (1 tsp) chopped fresh thyme
Grated peel of ½ orange
Salt and freshly ground black pepper to taste

VAN DER HUM SAUCE
Juice of 2 oranges
375 ml (1½ cups) reserved liquid from the casserole in which the birds were braised
60 ml (¼ cup) Van der Hum liqueur
60 ml (4 Tbsp) orange marmalade
Salt and freshly ground black pepper to taste

Stuffing: Melt the butter in a pan and sauté the onion and celery until just soft. Remove from the heat. Cool. Add the rest of the ingredients, mix well and stuff the guinea fowl. Truss the birds with string.

Preheat the oven to 160 °C. Heat a large pan and fry the bacon rashers until the fat begins to run. Then brown the guinea fowl all over in this fat (adding a little extra oil if necessary). Add the onion and carrot and cook for a few minutes. Carefully transfer the guinea fowl into a large casserole dish. Add the bacon and vegetables. Add the stock, orange juice, peel and Van der Hum. Cover and place in the oven for 2 hours, or until tender, adding a little more stock during the cooking process, if necessary. To crisp the skin of the guinea fowl, increase the oven temperature to 200 °C. Carefully transfer the birds from the casserole dish to a greased roasting pan and return to the hot oven for 10 minutes. Serve with the Van der Hum sauce (below) and roast potatoes and peas. **SERVES 6–8**

Sauce: Combine all the sauce ingredients in a saucepan and bring to the boil. Simmer for 20–30 minutes until reduced (thicken with cornflour if necessary). Adjust the seasoning and serve hot.

Stuffed Guinea Fowl with Van Der Hum Sauce

Rest, relax, unwind, taste the true Karoo

The Karoo's fine weather and clear skies make it the perfect place for braais (barbecues). There's nothing to compare with sitting round an open fire, particularly at night when the stars seem only a breath away in the crystal-clear night skies. Normally as the meat begins to sizzle and tantalizing aromas fill the air, the stories start. The special atmosphere of a Karoo braai captivated drivers on the Zulu Tracbar outside Beaufort West in 2004, a rally open only to Citroëns manufactured between 1934 and 1957. They visited Hillandale Guest Farm, where a special traditional braai was laid on to entertain them. They were treated to liver and bacon rolls, lamb and pork chops, venison sausage, boerewors (farmer's sausage), chicken wings, vegetable potjie (stew prepared in a cast-iron pot) and an array of salads all made from home-grown ingredients. There was also an extensive table of home-made breads, jams and preserves, as well as koeksisters, small milk tarts, home-made chunky fudge and quince sweets for dessert. The group so enjoyed their open-air feast that a repeat performance was arranged for breakfast. The jams and preserves on the bread table were joined by wild honey and a variety of home-made marmalades. Creamy mealie meal porridge, cooked over the coals, was served with fresh full-cream farm milk, stewed fruit, egg, bacon, sausages, fried home-grown tomatoes and fritters made from garden spinach. Fortunately the cars did not have to travel in a convoy because many of the drivers decided to linger longer and soak up this Karoo hospitality.

Braai

Near Merweville, in the Great Karoo, nature dazzles on endless plains and blue mountains link the earth to the sky.

LAMB SOSATIES

4 legs of lamb, de-boned and cut into cubes

CURRY SAUCE
Butter or oil for frying
2 large onions, sliced
60 ml (4 Tbsp) curry powder
30 ml (2 Tbsp) turmeric
90 ml (6 Tbsp) sugar
60 ml (4 Tbsp) cornflour
500 ml (2 cups) water
750 ml (3 cups) vinegar
500 ml (2 cups) fruit chutney
250 ml (1 cup) medium cream sherry
Salt and freshly ground black pepper to taste

Weigh the cubes of meat – this is important so that the amount of salt to be added can be calculated.

Curry sauce: Heat the butter or oil in a pan. Fry the onions until softened. Stir in the curry powder, turmeric, sugar and cornflour. Add the water, vinegar and chutney and bring to the boil. Simmer for a few minutes. Cool before adding the sherry.

Pour the cold curry mixture over the cubed meat and marinate in the refrigerator for 2–3 days. Sprinkle with salt (10 ml (2 tsp) per 500 g of meat) and pepper. Stir the mixture every day.

After the meat has marinated for a few days, thread the cubes onto skewers – placing about 6 cubes on each skewer. Grill over hot coals. Bring the sauce to the boil and cook rapidly for about 2 minutes. Thicken slightly if necessary and serve this as well as some additional chutney with the sosaties. **MAKES 30–36**

CRUMBED LAMB'S TAILS

Anyone wanting to try out this special dish could order lamb's tails from their local butcher. On farms, as the tails are docked they are collected and plunged into boiling water so that the wool can be pulled off.

3–4 lamb's tails per person
Salt and freshly ground black pepper to taste
2–3 eggs
Dried breadcrumbs

If the butcher has not already done this, prepare the tails for cooking by removing most of the fat. Place them in a saucepan. Cover with water, add salt and pepper to taste and simmer until the tails are tender – about 1½–2 hours.

In a bowl beat the eggs until the yolks and whites are well mixed. Place some breadcrumbs in a plastic packet. Dip the tails into the egg mixture and one by one shake them around in the plastic bag until each is well coated with crumbs. Place the tails in the refrigerator for at least 1 hour before braaiing them on the coals until crisp and delicious.

SKILPADJIES (LAMB'S LIVER IN CAUL FAT) – TRADITIONAL VERSION

500 g lamb's liver
Milk for soaking
Caul fat (the stringy fat that surrounds the stomach of sheep)
1 large onion, finely chopped
Salt and freshly ground black pepper to taste
Toothpicks

Remove any skin, membrane, veins or gristle from the liver. Soak in milk for about 30 minutes to remove the bitterness. Drain. Cut the liver into long strips. Cut the caul fat into similar-sized strips (so that each will cover a strip of liver when it is folded over). Place one strip of caul fat onto a working surface, put a strip of liver on top of it and sprinkle this with a little of the finely chopped onion. Fold both the caul fat and liver into a little sausage shape and fasten with a toothpick. Sprinkle with salt and pepper or braai spice or salt. Braai over hot coals. **SERVES 5**

Lamb Sosaties

Karoo 'Oysters' with Wild Mushrooms and Red Wine Sauce

KAROO 'OYSTERS' WITH WILD MUSHROOMS AND RED WINE SAUCE

500 g lamb's liver
Milk for soaking
500 g caul fat, soaked overnight in cold water to cover
Salt and freshly ground black pepper to taste
50 g large sage leaves

WILD MUSHROOMS
500 g (1 large or 2 small punnets) fresh porcini or large field mushrooms (or a mixture of both)
30 ml (2 Tbsp) olive oil
20 ml (4 tsp) butter
Salt and freshly ground black pepper to taste
5 ml (1 tsp) lemon juice
2 cloves garlic, finely chopped
5 ml (1 tsp) chopped fresh thyme
25 ml (5 tsp) chopped fresh flat-leaf parsley

RED WINE SAUCE
30 ml (2 Tbsp) olive oil
1 medium onion, chopped
1 medium carrot, peeled and chopped
½ stick celery, chopped
750 ml (1 bottle) good red wine
750 ml (3 cups) chicken stock
2 sprigs each thyme, parsley and sage
100 g butter
Salt, freshly ground black pepper and sugar to taste

Liver: Remove any skin, membrane, veins or gristle from the liver. Soak in milk for about 30 minutes to remove the bitterness. Drain. Trim the liver and slice into four equal steaks. Carefully unravel the caul fat and divide into four equal portions. Season the liver with salt and pepper. Place a sage leaf in the centre of each piece of caul and centre a piece of liver on top of the leaf. Wrap this into a parcel, covering twice with the fat. Set aside in a cool place until needed.

Wild mushrooms: Wipe the mushrooms with a damp cloth and slice thickly. If using porcini, peel the stems with a potato peeler before slicing. Heat the olive oil in a large pan and, when hot, sauté the mushrooms for about 3 minutes, tossing regularly, then add the butter. Season with salt and pepper to taste and add the lemon juice, garlic and thyme. Keep warm. Add the parsley just before serving, tossing to combine.

Red wine sauce: In a large pot, heat the oil over medium high heat. Add the onion, carrot and celery and cook, stirring regularly, until tender (about 8 minutes). Add the wine, bring to the boil, and skim any froth that rises to the surface. Boil rapidly to reduce until only 60 ml (¼ cup) of liquid remains. Add the stock and the herbs and reduce again by two-thirds. Strain into a clean pot, pressing on the solids to release their juices. Discard the solids. Bring the sauce to the boil, reduce the heat to a simmer and whisk the butter into the sauce (about 25 ml (5 tsp) at a time). Season with salt and pepper, using a pinch of sugar to correct any excessive bitterness in the sauce. Keep warm.

Cook the Karoo Oysters over an open fire until medium (this will take about 2 minutes per side). By then the caul fat will have mostly rendered away and the sage leaf will be clearly visible. Serve on top of the mushrooms. Garnish with a sage leaf and pour the sauce around the mushrooms. **SERVES 4**

Note: This recipe was specially developed for this publication by Peter Pankhurst, chef at the Savoy Cabbage, widely known for offal and traditional dishes and 'an extension of the Karoo in Cape Town'. The 'oysters' can also be pan-fried and served on a bed of buttered spinach or chard to ring the changes.

$\mathcal{L}$AMB GULLET WITH CURRIED PRICKLY PEAR LEAVES

500 g young prickly pear leaves
Blue copperas (blue stone, blue vitriol, copper
sulphate) or 30 ml (2 Tbsp) bicarbonate of soda
2–4 lamb's gullets (rooislukderm), cleaned

CURRY SAUCE
100 g butter
3 onions, chopped
10 cloves garlic, crushed
25 ml (5 tsp) curry powder
25 ml (5 tsp) mustard powder
500 ml (2 cups) vinegar
10 ml (2 tsp) salt
25 ml (5 tsp) golden syrup
250 ml (1 cup) sugar
100 ml (a bit under ½ cup) cornflour, mixed to
a paste with cold water

Choose young prickly pear leaves on which the thorns have not yet fully developed, but appear as 'rubbery' bumps. (Wear gloves anyway.) Holding the leaves at the cut end and using a blunt knife, scrape them as if you were scaling a fish. Rinse the leaves quickly under running water (do not leave them lying in the water). Then, using a sharp knife, cut right around each leaf to remove their edges and the hard portion where they were attached to the mother plant. Now, cut them into thin strips. Cook the strips in boiling water to which you have added a grain of blue copperas to keep the nice green colour. Cook for about 20 minutes, or until tender. Strain.

Curry sauce: Heat the butter and sauté the onions and garlic until softened. Stir in the curry and mustard powders and cook for 1 minute. Add the remaining sauce ingredients, except the cornflour paste, bring to a simmer, then remove from the heat. Add the paste and return to the heat and cook, stirring, until the sauce thickens. Stir in the prickly pear strips. Fill the lamb gullets with the mixture, but do not stuff too tightly. Tie the ends with a piece of string then submerge the gullets in boiling water and simmer until they are tender. Drain, cool and freeze if desired.

Braai over medium coals until the skins are crisp and the filling is heated through. Serve with other braaied meats. **SERVES 4–6**

Note: This prickly pear sauce is quite delicious. It can be bottled and used whenever needed, as an accompaniment to any meat dish. It is also excellent on its own as a salad. In Spain prickly pear leaves are prepared in a similar way and called *nopalitos*.

$\mathcal{S}$OUTRIBBETJIE (SALTED MUTTON RIB)

30 ml (2 Tbsp) brown sugar
250 g salt
2.5 ml (½ tsp) saltpetre
1.5–2 kg mutton rib
Lemon juice for sprinkling

Mix the sugar, salt and saltpetre together. Rub the dry ingredients well into the meat. Leave in the refrigerator for 2 days. Remove the meat from the brine and hang in a draft until dry on the outside. Cover with cold water and bring to the boil. Reduce the heat and simmer for 1½–2 hours, or until the meat is almost tender. Remove from the liquid and hang in a cool place to dry. Grill slowly over coals, cut into portions and serve sprinkled with lemon juice. **SERVES 4–6**

CURRIED PORK CHOPS

± 8 lean pork chops

CURRY MARINADE
1 kg onions, chopped
15 ml (1 Tbsp) salt
25 ml (5 tsp) curry powder
15 ml (1 Tbsp) turmeric
2.5 ml (½ tsp) freshly ground black pepper
250 ml (1 cup) red wine
500 ml (2 cups) vinegar
250 g (1 packet) dried apricots
75 ml (5 Tbsp) smooth apricot jam

Mix all ingredients for the curry marinade together in a saucepan. Heat gently and simmer slowly for about 7 minutes. Set aside until cold. Place the chops in this marinade and marinate in the refrigerator for 2–3 days. Turn regularly. Braai over hot coals. **SERVES 4–6**

Note: Try making these chops just before you leave for a holiday – they last well in a cool bag. This will ensure you can have a delicious braai and taste of home, soon after arriving at your holiday destination.

Curried Pork Chops

Ostrich Sosaties with Peanut Sauce

OSTRICH SOSATIES WITH PEANUT SAUCE

500 g ostrich fillet or steak, cut into cubes
300 g small brown mushrooms, wiped clean
Pieces of yellow, green and red pepper
150 ml (just under ⅔ cup) coconut milk
50 ml (just over 3 Tbsp) beef stock
30 ml (2 Tbsp) chopped fresh coriander
30 ml (2 Tbsp) brown sugar
20 ml (4 tsp) red (Thai) curry paste
50 ml (just over 3 Tbsp) (Thai) fish sauce
20 ml (4 tsp) oil
5 ml (1 tsp) coriander seeds, bruised

PEANUT SAUCE (MAKE IN ADVANCE)
10 ml (2 tsp) oil
1 onion, finely chopped
1 clove garlic, crushed
2.5 ml (½ tsp) ground cumin
2.5 ml (½ tsp) curry paste
50 ml (just over 3 Tbsp) peanut butter
150 ml (just under ⅔ cup) coconut milk
15 ml (1 Tbsp) brown sugar
10 ml (2 tsp) lemon juice
10 ml (2 tsp) (Thai) fish sauce
30 ml (2 Tbsp) roasted peanuts, finely chopped
100 ml (a bit under ½ cup) chicken stock

Place the cubes of ostrich meat, the mushrooms and pieces of pepper into a bowl. Combine all the other ingredients, mix well and pour over the meat mixture. Marinate for 2–3 hours. Thread the meat, mushrooms and pepper pieces onto wooden or metal skewers. Braai over hot coals. **MAKES 6–8**

Peanut sauce: Heat the oil, add the onion and garlic and fry lightly. Add the cumin and curry paste and cook for a further 30 seconds. Stir in the peanut butter, coconut milk and brown sugar. Bring to the boil and simmer for 3 minutes. Add lemon juice, fish sauce and chopped peanuts. Bring to the boil, gently add chicken stock and boil until the mixture reaches the consistency of a dipping sauce. Serve hot with the sosaties. **MAKES ABOUT 400 ML**

TRADITIONAL KLIPRIB (STONE-BRAAIED RIB)

± 1.5 kg full rack sheep's rib
1 small pineapple, halved
Freshly ground black pepper
Freshly ground coriander
Salt to taste

Remove the breastbone and crack the ribs into two separate sections. Rub well with pineapple. Flavour with the freshly ground black pepper and coriander and sprinkle with a little salt before braaiing. **SERVES 10–12**

Note: Lawrence Green describes shepherds doing this in the Karoo. To make kliprib, similar-sized pieces of Karoo stone are balanced in an A-frame and a fire is built beneath them. The stones are slowly heated to red hot. Then the ribs are 'hung' across them – one on each side of the A – and left to sizzle for about 35 minutes until well done and crispy. This way of braaiing encompasses the essence of the unhurried lifestyle of the Karoo and allows plenty of time to enjoy the great outdoors and limitless spaces of the region. Traditionally this dish was served with samp, which burbled along in an iron pot over a separate fire.

MARINATED BRAAIED CHICKEN

1 x large chicken (± 1.5 kg), cleaned and cut into portions

MARINADE
375 ml (1½ cups) vinegar
25 ml (5 tsp) Worcestershire sauce
25 ml (5 tsp) tomato sauce
25 ml (5 tsp) soy sauce
30 ml (2 Tbsp) salt
15 ml (1 Tbsp) paprika
20 ml (4 tsp) mustard powder
15 ml (1 Tbsp) dried mixed herbs
10 ml (2 tsp) finely chopped onion
10 ml (2 tsp) garlic flakes
10 ml (2 tsp) zeal
10 ml (2 tsp) Tabasco
10 ml (2 tsp) chicken spice
250 ml (1 cup) oil

Mix all the marinade ingredients, except the oil. Gradually stir in the oil. Place the chicken pieces in this braai sauce to marinate for a few hours. Turn regularly. Place the chicken pieces over medium coals and cook slowly, using the marinade as a basting sauce while braaiing. Turn the chicken pieces frequently to prevent burning and to ensure even cooking. **SERVES 4–6**

'ASADO' BRAAI SAUCE

1 large onion, very finely chopped
12 cloves garlic, crushed
5 ml (1 tsp) ground coriander
5 ml (1 tsp) whole cloves, crushed
5 ml (1 tsp) black peppercorns, ground
2.5 ml (½ tsp) paprika
2.5 ml (½ tsp) cayenne pepper
85 g salt
60 ml (¼ cup) vinegar
500 ml (2 cups) water

Place all the ingredients in a large bottle. Seal well. Leave to stand for at least 10 days. Shake regularly to allow flavours to develop. Use as a basting sauce for braais, as a marinade, or add a dash to stews to pick them up. **MAKES ± 650 ML**

Note: This sauce was developed by the descendants of a group of farmers who emigrated to Argentina, with General Ben Viljoen, after the Anglo-Boer (South African) War.

A secluded by-way in the Great Karoo.

Salads and Side Dishes for Braais

A feast for the eyes and palate

Side dishes and salads are a fundamental part of a Karoo braai. Here good and adventurous cooks soar above the run-of-the-mill and traditional sousboontjies (saucy beans) rub shoulders with exotic taste adventures and palate teasers designed to complement the flavours of the meat. An American visitor on Alexanderkraal farm near Murraysburg district once claimed to be 'stunned' by 'Karoo home cookin''. After sampling all the side dishes at a braai he drawled: 'Lawdy-be, I believe I just died and went to heaven!'

Mustard Beans

4 large onions, sliced
2.5 kg green beans, topped, tailed and sliced
30 ml (2 Tbsp) salt
1.25 litres grape vinegar
1 kg sugar
125 ml (½ cup) cornflour
125 ml (½ cup) mustard powder
10 ml (2 tsp) turmeric
250 ml (1 cup) water

Place the onions, green beans and salt into a large saucepan with just enough boiling water to cover. Boil until the beans are just tender, but still crisp. Drain and cool. Slowly heat the grape vinegar and sugar until the sugar dissolves. Mix the cornflour, mustard powder and turmeric with the water and add to the vinegar mixture. Add the drained beans and heat slowly until the sauce comes to the boil and thickens. Stir constantly to ensure the mixture does not burn. Check seasoning and serve hot or cold. **SERVES 8–10**

Note: Traditionally, green beans are made with a curry sauce. This is a delightfully different and tasty variation. Both versions keep well if bottled in sterilized jars while hot.

Slaphaksteentjies (Onions in Sweet-and-Sour Sauce)

1.2 kg small (pickling) onions
250 ml (1 cup) water
125 ml (½ cup) vinegar
175 ml (just under ¾ cup) sugar
12.5 ml (2½ tsp) cornflour
5 ml (1 tsp) mustard powder
1 ml (¼ tsp) salt
1 egg, beaten
12.5 ml (2½ tsp) butter

Peel the onions but do not cut the ends off, and boil in salted water until tender. Drain and set aside in a bowl. Place the 250 ml (1 cup) water in a pot and add the vinegar. In a bowl, mix the sugar, cornflour, mustard powder and salt together. Add the egg, and then add this to the water and vinegar mixture. Slowly bring to the boil, add butter and pour the hot sauce over the onions. Leave to cool. This onion salad will keep well in the refrigerator for about a week. **SERVES 8–10**

Roosterkoek (Griddle Cakes)

4 x 10 g packets instant dry yeast
20 ml (4 tsp) sugar
5 kg white bread flour
20 ml (4 tsp) salt
3 litres lukewarm water
250 g butter or margarine

Dissolve the yeast and sugar in a little warm water. Add a little flour and leave to rise for about 5 minutes. Knead this sour dough mixture into the rest of the flour and salt, adding lukewarm water as needed to form a firm dough. Then add the butter or margarine and knead until the mixture no longer sticks to your hands. Cover and set aside for 20 minutes to rise.

Knock back the dough and form into long sausages on a floured surface. Flatten slightly and cut into pieces. Set these aside on a greased baking sheet and leave for 5–10 minutes to rise again. Then bake them over 'cool' coals at the braai fire. As soon as they are done, remove from the grid and rub the crusts with a little butter if you do not wish these to become too crisp. The cooked griddle cakes can be frozen and reheated as required. **MAKES ABOUT 10 DOZEN (120)**

Beetroot in Raisin Sauce

12.5 ml (2½ tsp) cornflour
25 ml (5 tsp) sugar
1 ml (¼ tsp) salt
125 ml (½ cup) water
500 ml (2 cups) cooked and cubed beetroot
125 ml (½ cup) seedless raisins
75 ml (5 Tbsp) vinegar
15 ml (1 Tbsp) butter or margarine

Place the cornflour, sugar, salt and water into a saucepan. Heat, stirring all the time over a medium heat until the sauce thickens and becomes clear. Add the rest of the ingredients, stir and heat through. Scoop into a serving bowl and cool. **SERVES 4–6**

Brinjal (Aubergine) Salad

2 brinjals (aubergines)
60 ml (4 Tbsp) mayonnaise
3 hard-boiled eggs, chopped
15 ml (1 Tbsp) chopped fresh parsley
1 medium onion, chopped
1 clove garlic, crushed
30 ml (2 Tbsp) olive oil
30 ml (2 Tbsp) lemon juice
5 ml (1 tsp) salt
2.5 ml (½ tsp) freshly ground black pepper

Preheat the oven to 180 °C. Make slits in the aubergines and bake in the oven for about 30 minutes until soft. Cool. Scoop out all the flesh and lightly mix into the other ingredients. Garnish with extra parsley. **SERVES 4–6**

QUICK AND EASY ROOSTERKOEK (GRIDDLE CAKES)

500 ml (2 cups) cake flour
10 ml (2 tsp) baking powder
Salt to taste
250 ml (1 cup) fresh cream

Sift the dry ingredients into a mixing bowl. Add the cream. Knead and divide into little squares. Grill both sides on a hot griddle pan until each square is well cooked through. Serve warm with farm butter (if possible) and home-made preserves.
MAKES 10–15

Roosterkoek, Slaphaksteentjies and Mustard Beans

CABBAGE FILLED WITH SAMP

1 large cabbage
10 ml (2 tsp) oil
1 onion, finely sliced
2 cloves garlic, crushed
1 chilli, de-seeded and chopped (optional)
125 g (½ packet) diced bacon (or sufficient to flavour the samp)
30 ml (2 Tbsp) butter
30 ml (2 Tbsp) cake flour
250 ml (1 cup) milk
Salt and freshly ground black pepper to taste
250 ml (1 cup) cooked samp (sufficient to fill ¾ of the cabbage when it is hollowed out)
250 ml (1 cup) cubed mature Cheddar cheese

Wash the cabbage, remove any damaged outside leaves and neatly cut off the stem. Cut a 'lid' section off at the top and then, using a sharp knife, hollow out the cabbage.

Filling: Heat the oil and sauté the onion, garlic and chilli. Add the bacon and fry until crisp. Melt the butter in a separate saucepan, add the flour and stir to make a roux. Slowly add the milk and bring to the boil to make a thick white sauce. Check seasoning. Place the samp in a bowl; add the bacon and onion mix, the cheese and sufficient white sauce to ensure a moist, but not sloppy filling for the cabbage. Scoop this mixture into the hollowed-out cabbage. Place its 'lid' on top and seal well and tightly in tin foil. (Be sure that you know where the top is. Also be sure that the cabbage is sealed tightly enough for the 'lid' not to slide off or become loose while it is cooking. This is essential because the cabbage has to be turned throughout the cooking process.)

As soon as the braai fire is ready, place the cabbage on the grid over the coals. Turn regularly. When ready, the cabbage will feel soft when pressed. Remove from the coals and place on a serving tray, with the 'lid'-side uppermost. Open the foil, remove the lid and serve. **SERVES 4–6**

Prickly pears, a tasty treat enjoyed by man and beast, are also used to distill powerful liquor.

Vegetable Potjie

700 g potatoes
1 medium onion
2 carrots
350 g sweet potatoes
150 g green beans
350 g butternut
Cabbage
1 packet white onion soup powder
250 g butter, melted

Layer the vegetables, except cabbage, in a three-legged cast-iron pot in the order given. Mix the onion soup powder and melted butter and pour over the vegetables. Do not add water. Make a 'lid' with thick cabbage leaves. Cover the pot with its own tight-fitting lid and cook very slowly for about 1 hour over 'cool' or very few coals. **SERVES 6–8**

Pap (Mealie Meal) and Spinach Tart

PAP
1 litre (4 cups) milk
15 ml (1 Tbsp) butter
5 ml (1 tsp) salt
500 ml (2 cups) mealie meal (braaipap)
1 x 420 g can creamed sweetcorn

FILLING
10 ml (2 tsp) oil
250 g (1 packet) bacon, chopped
1 large onion, finely chopped
2 cloves garlic, finely chopped
250 g (1 punnet) button mushrooms, wiped clean and sliced (use more mushrooms if desired)
3 tomatoes, chopped
1 x 250–300 g packet ready-made creamed spinach with feta
Salt and freshly ground black pepper to taste
Grated nutmeg (optional)
125–250 ml (½–1 cup) grated Cheddar cheese
125 ml (½ cup) fresh cream or evaporated milk

Pap: Bring the milk to the boil, add the butter, salt and mealie meal and simmer over a medium heat, stirring now and then, until cooked. Take care not to burn the mixture. When done, remove from the heat and stir in the sweetcorn. Divide the cooked mealie meal into three equal parts and shape into rounds by pressing each into a loose-bottomed pan or onto three similar-sized plates. Set aside to cool.

Filling: While the mealie meal is cooking, heat the oil in a saucepan. Fry the bacon until crisp. Add the onion, garlic and mushrooms and fry until softened. In a separate pan, fry the tomatoes in oil and, when done, add to the onion, bacon, garlic and mushroom mix. Add the creamed spinach and feta. Mix well and add seasoning and nutmeg. Set aside to cool.

Once the mealie meal rounds have cooled, heat the oven to 180 °C. Place one mealie meal round into an ovenproof dish or deep, round 23 cm springform pan. Spread with about one-third of the bacon mixture. Sprinkle with one-third grated cheese. Carefully place the second mealie meal round on top of this. Spread again with the bacon mix and top with cheese. Repeat this with the third round. Carefully pour cream or evaporated milk over these rounds and bake in the oven for 30–45 minutes. Serve hot, sliced into wedges. **SERVES 10–12**

Home grown adds zest and inner meaning

Karoo people mostly grow their own vegetables and even town gardens have *groente akkertjies* (vegetable plots). Freshly picked vegetables are full of flavour and this is a feature of Karoo cuisine. Tomatoes, spinach, green beans, carrots, turnips, sweet potatoes, parsnips and pumpkin all grow easily in the Karoo and so form the basis of most traditional tasty bredies and stews. Early cooks of the arid zone could not easily find herbs and spices to liven up their dishes, so some experimented with wild herbs, which gave Karoo dishes a special flavour all of their own. Today, special projects run by the previously disadvantaged communities ensure herbs are easy to find. Beaufort West Hydroponics supplies a range of fresh herbs and Leeu-Gamka Koup Knoffel produces top quality garlic. Most Karoo cooks agree with the epicurean philosopher, Martin Versveld, who claimed that 'herbs do for your dishes what grace does for your actions – gives them zest and inner meaning'.

From the earliest days in the Karoo, far-flung farmsteads have played a fundamental role in providing hospitality and fine food.

Vegetables

PUMPKIN TART

500 ml (2 cups) cooked pumpkin (1 kg raw pumpkin, cut into pieces)
60 ml (4 Tbsp) sugar
45 ml (3 Tbsp) butter
2 eggs
80 ml (⅓ cup) cake flour
5 ml (1 tsp) baking powder
Salt
80 ml (⅓ cup) milk
Grated nutmeg, ground cloves and ground cinnamon to taste

Mash the pumpkin until smooth. Cool. Preheat the oven to 180 °C. Beat sugar and butter to a creamy consistency, and then add the eggs, one by one, and continue beating. Sift the flour, baking powder and salt together and add, alternately with the milk, to the egg mixture. Add the cooked pumpkin. (Do not stir the mixture too much.) Spoon the mixture into a greased baking pan measuring approximately 20 x 28 cm and sprinkle with the spices. Bake in the oven for 30–45 minutes.
SERVES 6–8

Pumpkin Tart

PATATS (SWEET POTATOES)

1.5 litres (6 cups) water
2 cinnamon sticks
15 ml (1 Tbsp) butter
1 kg (4 or 5) sweet potatoes, peeled and cubed
Custard powder to thicken

Place the water in a saucepan and add the cinnamon and butter. Bring to the boil. Add the sweet potatoes and cook until soft. Remove the cinnamon sticks and thicken with custard powder mixed to a paste with a little water. Cook through and scoop the mixture into an attractive dish for serving. **SERVES 4–6**

Note: Author Lawrence Green said sweet potatoes were revered in the hinterland to a degree unknown in the towns. This may well be true. A leafy green patch of sweet potatoes (*patats*) will be found in virtually every vegetable garden and once a good variety is obtained the *ranke*, or shoots, are jealously guarded. Sweet potatoes are baked, boiled, fried, chipped, used in curries or turned into delicious side dishes by adding sugar, cinnamon, naartjie juice or orange peel.

BAKED SPINACH

750 ml (3 cups) cooked and finely chopped spinach

SAUCE
60 ml (4 Tbsp) butter
60 ml (4 Tbsp) cake flour
375 ml (1½ cups) milk
3 eggs
Salt and freshly ground black pepper to taste
1 ring (± 50 g) feta cheese

Preheat the oven to 180 °C. Make a white sauce with the butter, flour and milk. Beat the eggs lightly and add to white sauce. Season to taste. Add the feta cheese. Add the finely chopped spinach to this mixture. Pour into a buttered ovenproof dish and place in a pan of hot water in the oven. Bake for 30 minutes until puffed up and slightly brown on top. **SERVES 4–6**

CREAMED SPINACH

1 kg fresh spinach
30 ml (2 Tbsp) butter
30 ml (2 Tbsp) cake flour
5 ml (1 tsp) garlic and herb seasoning
500 ml (2 cups) milk
Salt and freshly ground black pepper to taste
125 ml (½ cup) thick fresh cream

Wash the spinach and remove the stalks. Pack the leaves in a large saucepan. Do not add any water, as the moisture remaining on the leaves after washing will be sufficient to steam the spinach. Cover and cook until just soft – 3–5 minutes. Remove from the pot and drain. While draining, melt the butter and make a roux with the flour. Add the garlic and herb seasoning, and then gradually add the milk to form a thick sauce. Chop the spinach and add to the sauce. Season. Reheat, and then stir in the cream just before serving. Do not boil as the spinach will discolour and the cream will curdle. **SERVES 4–6**

Butternut Supreme

Butternut Supreme

2 large butternut
10 ml (2 tsp) olive oil
2 large onions, finely chopped
2 brinjals (aubergines), skinned and
finely chopped
125 ml (½ cup) sliced brown mushrooms
250 ml (1 cup) frozen green peas
2 cooked potatoes, cubed
2 Russian sausages, finely chopped
Salt and freshly ground black pepper to taste
Grated mature Cheddar cheese for topping

Preheat the oven to 180 °C. Cut the butternuts in half and take out the pips. Put the halves into a large pot with water and salt and cook for about 15 minutes. Remove with a slotted spoon, and carefully scrape the flesh out of the skins. Keep the flesh to one side. Place the shells upside down on a tray to drain – take great care, as they are soft and may break. Lightly sprinkle salt over the brinjals, leave for 20 minutes and then rinse off.

Heat the oil in a pan and fry the onions until softened. Add the butternut flesh, brinjals and mushrooms and cook until soft – about 15 minutes. Cook the peas in a separate pot, drain and add. Stir in the potato cubes. Add the sausage and seasoning. Place the butternut skins right side up on a greased baking sheet. Divide the vegetable mixture into four and scoop some into each shell. Top with grated cheese and place in the oven. Bake for a few minutes to reheat and allow the cheese to melt. Serve hot. **SERVES 4**

Sweet Cauliflower

1 medium cauliflower, chopped
3 eggs
200 ml (just over ¾ cup) sugar
250 ml (1 cup) milk
15 ml (1 Tbsp) custard powder
Salt and freshly ground black pepper to taste
10 ml (2 tsp) baking powder
Grated nutmeg for dusting
Butter to dot on top

Preheat the oven to 180 °C. Cook the cauliflower in boiling water until soft. Drain. Beat the eggs and sugar well together, and then add the milk, custard power, salt and pepper. Add the cauliflower and the baking powder. Mix well. Sprinkle with nutmeg, turn into a greased ovenproof bowl and dot with butter. Bake in the oven for 30–45 minutes until golden brown on top. **SERVES 4–6**

Baked Marrow

1 large marrow, peeled and cubed
5 ml (1 tsp) ground cinnamon

SAUCE
375 ml (1½ cups) sugar
15 ml (1 Tbsp) butter
50 ml (just over 3 Tbsp) cake flour
5 ml (1 tsp) baking powder
4 eggs, well beaten
250 ml (1 cup) milk

Preheat the oven to 180 °C. Cook the marrow in boiling salted water until just tender. Drain and spread evenly into a greased ovenproof dish.

Sauce: Beat all the sauce ingredients together until well combined and pour over the marrow cubes. Sprinkle cinnamon over the top and bake in the oven for 45–60 minutes until set. **SERVES 6–8**

GARLICKY VEGETABLE MEDLEY

20 ml (4 tsp) olive oil
20 ml (4 tsp) butter
1 red onion, thinly sliced into rings
4 cloves garlic, crushed
250 ml (1 cup) sweetcorn kernels
2 gem squash, de-pipped, removed from shell
and cut into small cubes
4 baby marrows (courgettes), sliced
A handful young green beans, finely sliced
4 young carrots, julienned
125 ml (½ cup) chicken stock
Cornflour to thicken
45 ml (3 Tbsp) chopped fresh parsley
30 ml (2 Tbsp) butter
Salt and freshly ground black pepper to taste

Heat the oil and butter in a saucepan until the butter begins to froth. Add the onion and garlic and sauté. Add all the vegetables and stir-fry for a few minutes until their aromas begin to rise. Gently add the chicken stock, cover and simmer for 10–15 minutes until the vegetables are just tender. Thicken any sauce that remains with a little cornflour mixed with cold water. Simmer until the sauce is translucent and adds a shine to the vegetables. Turn into a serving dish. Mix the parsley and butter together and dot across the hot vegetables. Add a pinch of freshly ground black pepper and serve. **SERVES 4–6**

TEMPTING POTATO CAKE

60 g butter
4 large onions, finely chopped
6 large potatoes, peeled, thinly sliced and cut
into matchsticks
1 x 45 g can anchovies in oil
Salt and freshly ground black pepper to taste
250 ml (1 cup) fresh cream
30 ml (2 Tbsp) fresh breadcrumbs
60 ml (4 Tbsp) grated Cheddar cheese
30 ml (2 Tbsp) finely chopped fresh parsley

Preheat the oven to 200 °C. Heat the butter and sauté the onions until translucent. Remove from the heat. Pat the potatoes with strips of paper towel to remove their moisture. When dry, place the potato strips in a greased casserole dish with the fried onions and the anchovies and their oil. Season to taste and stir lightly to combine. Pour over half the cream and bake in the oven for 15 minutes. Remove from the oven, and reduce the heat to 180 °C. Pour the rest of the cream over the potatoes. Mix the breadcrumbs, cheese and parsley together and sprinkle this over the top. Return to the oven for a further 20–30 minutes, or until the potatoes are soft, the cream has been absorbed and the top is golden brown. Serve hot. **SERVES 4–6**

Note: An intriguing legend surrounds this dish. It is said that way back a religious zealot foreswore all earthly pleasures and embarked on a hunger strike. One day he caught a whiff of this potato cake. The aroma alone was sufficient to change his mind.

Garlicky Vegetable Medley

Distinctive, mouthwatering flavours

Bread was not easy to find in the old Karoo, as flour, yeast and rising agents were difficult to obtain. But farmers' wives soon learned the art of grinding meal between stones and making their own yeast from sour dough, potatoes or veld plants. Prince Albert historian Pat Marincowitz says early pioneers cooked outdoors using hollowed-out ant heaps. Brick or clay ovens with chimneys and doors were built later. The ovens were built outside, but with doors inside the kitchen so that 'rising pans' and bread could easily be put into the oven and taken out again. Getting the oven temperature right was an art. A fire, mostly of mimosa wood, was made inside the oven and kept going until the required heat was attained. Ashes were then scraped out and the bread placed inside. Outdoor oven doors were sealed – mostly with mud – and when the seal was broken crispy bread emerged to be rubbed with butter and covered with a blanket to cool. Experts say the unique flavour of this bread came from the yeasts, microscopic dust particles and trace elements emitted by the millstones. 'Early bread pans were over 15 cm deep and bread rose about 7 cm above their rims,' says Pat. 'Pioneer women clasped these huge 22 cm loaves to their chests and cut thick slices from them using long, sharp knives – a feat no woman would dare today.' In *The Plains of the Camdeboo*, Eve Palmer said Karoo bread always had a faint taste of mimosa, even when cool. In 1890 Anne Martin, in *Home Life on an Ostrich Farm*, urged settlers to learn to bake bread 'in the Boer way', and not to accept any 'old fly-infested offering' that came their way. 'If there ever was a competition for bread-makers of all countries in the world the Dutch women of the Karoo would bear away all the prizes for their delicious whole-meal bread, leavened with sour dough,' she said. Rusks are an essential part of Karoo culture. They were *padkos* for any journey, *veldkos* (bush food) for men tending the flocks and they were sent to boarding schools around the country to keep children in touch with home.

Breads and
Tea-time Treats

Old man-made 'sculptures', like this one near Prince Albert,
add intrigue to the pristine scenery of the Karoo.

OLIVE BREAD

500 g white bread flour

1 x 10 g packet active dry yeast (1 x 25 g cube
fresh yeast is preferable, if available)

250 ml (1 cup) lukewarm water

75 ml (5 Tbsp) olive oil

10 ml (2 tsp) salt

30 ml (2 Tbsp) chopped olives (spiced olives,
such as those made at Swartrivier farm in
Prince Albert, can be used to give this bread a
different, more savoury character)

15 ml (1 Tbsp) chopped fresh rosemary

15 ml (1 Tbsp) chopped fresh thyme

5 ml (1 tsp) crushed garlic

Coarse salt for topping

Place a little flour in a bowl. Make a well in the centre; add the yeast and enough lukewarm water to make a handful of dough. Cover and leave for 15 minutes in a warm place. Mix the rest of the water and flour into this mixture. Add the olive oil and salt and knead until soft, but not sticky. Place the dough in a bowl, cover and set aside in a warm place for 2 hours, until it has doubled in size. Then knead again, but take care not to press out all the air. Add the olives, rosemary and thyme. Form into a long or round loaf, or press the dough out into a baking pan and press your fingers into the top to make shallow dips to give it 'texture' when it's baked. Decorate with a few additional chopped olives, a sprig of rosemary and some crushed garlic and top with coarse salt. Cover and leave in a warm place for 30 minutes to rise. Preheat the oven to 200 °C. When the bread has risen, place in the oven and bake for 15–20 minutes until brown and cooked through. **MAKES 1 LOAF**

Note: This recipe, which originally comes from Italy, is a prizewinner of the Prince Albert Olive Festival. The bread freezes well. Simply defrost and reheat in an oven or under a grill before serving. The bread is also delicious if cut horizontally, filled with slices of melting cheese, tied together and reheated for 5–10 minutes. The earliest farmers were not enthusiastic about olives. They had to wait six or seven years for a crop and there seemed no market for olive oil. So in the beginning olives were generally regarded as pig or turkey food. Over the years that changed and by 1907 South Africa won a gold medal for producing the finest and purest olive oil within the British Empire. Today olive groves flourish across the Karoo, producing top quality oil and olive products.

The Art of Yeast-Making

Making suurdeeg (sourdough or yeast) was an art all of its own, says Pat Marincowitz. 'To start it off a potato was peeled, grated and boiled in about 1 litre of water for 10–20 minutes with ½ tablespoon of salt, 2 teaspoons of sugar, 2 or 3 raisins, and a slice of bread from a previous batch. Two or three cups of flour were sprinkled over this and pressed down. The pot was then left, normally overnight, in a warm place, between feather pillows or eiderdowns or in a cupboard. By the next day little bubbles and a yeasty aroma had developed. This mixture was beaten. Flour was added, the dough kneaded and left to rise. Ou suurdeeg was the first "dried yeast". When making bread, a handful of kneaded dough was pinched off and placed under the flour in the meal bin. When needed this was soaked in lukewarm water and kneaded to a dough again with flour. The longevity of this yeast was never tested because bread was always being baked and pinch-off bits of dough constantly saved for the next batch. Then there was the fickle "potato yeast", commonly called plantjie suurdeeg. For this, water, flour, grated potato, a tablespoon of sugar (preferably brown) and a cup of flour were put into a screw-top jar and left for two to three days in a warm place to ferment. A little was always held back for the next batch.' In today's world a 'friendship cake' based on this kind of yeast still does the rounds.

Olive Bread

POT BREAD

1 kg white bread flour
20 ml (4 tsp) salt
10 ml (2 tsp) sugar
1 x 10 g packet instant dried yeast
65 g butter
650 ml (just under 2⅔ cups) lukewarm water
1 egg, beaten

Combine the flour, salt and sugar and add the yeast. Add the butter and rub in. Add the water gradually and mix to form a soft dough. Knead well for 10 minutes. Place on a lightly floured surface and cover with clingfilm. Leave for 20 minutes. Knock back dough, shape into a ball and place in a well-greased, flat-bottomed cast-iron pot (see note below) that has a well-fitting lid. Cover and allow to rise again for 20–25 minutes. Preheat the oven to 180 °C. Brush with beaten egg and bake in the oven for 45 minutes or until the loaf sounds hollow when tapped.
MAKES 1 LOAF

Note: Getting pot bread out of its pot without breaking is easier than you'd think, says Pat Marincowitz. It has to be made in two pieces. One part fills ⁸⁄₁₀ of the pot. Flour is then sprinkled over this and a small half-moon of bread is then pressed into the remainder of the pot. After baking the pot is shaken and the small bread comes out first, freeing the larger one.

Armmansbrood (Poor Man's Bread)

Armmansbrood, gebraaidepap (braaied porridge) or waterbrood (water bread) were traditional taste treats of the old Karoo. All that was needed was flour, water and a little salt. These were mixed together and kneaded into a stiff dough. This was then rolled out (normally using a bottle) and then spread with hard fat or olive oil. The dough was then rolled up and rolled out again. This process was repeated four or five times until the fat and oil made the dough quite soft. Then it was finally rolled out to a thickness of about 10 mm and cut into slices – as large as today's bread slices – and 'baked' until crisp and golden brown over an open fire. 'Armmansbrood had a wonderful mealy flavour and was delicious with freshly brewed ground coffee and braaied meat,' says Pat Marincowitz. 'This bread has layers that can be peeled off, just like flaky pastry.'

The Magic of Fresh Farm Butter

Butter making is an art. City folk consider it tedious until they witness the magic. 'The cream is stored in pails and the fresh cream must never be mixed with the older lot until the second day, when it is mixed in well and stirred with a large wooden spoon or paddle,' says Joan Southey in Footprints in the Karoo. *The cream is left to stand in a really cool place. If it's hot, the pail is stood in a basin of cold water with a cloth draped over it. This reaches right down into the water and it's amazing how cool it keeps the cream. The liquid is stirred twice a day, until it becomes thick and develops a rich golden colour. 'That's when it's ready to churn,' says Joan, who simply beats the cream with a wooden spoon or paddle until 'the texture changes from velvety smooth to crumbly'. Then the butter quite suddenly separates itself from the buttermilk. All the buttermilk has to be squeezed out before the butter is washed in cold water, salted and moulded for use. And, of course, the residual buttermilk is used for puddings, fruit breads and rusks.*

BUTTERMILK HEALTH RUSKS

1 kg self-raising flour
500 ml (2 cups) wholewheat flour
15 ml (1 Tbsp) baking powder
5 x 250 ml (5 cups) raisin bran cereal
250 ml (1 cup) seedless raisins
250 ml (1 cup) chopped nuts of choice, i.e. walnuts, pecans, but preferably not peanuts
500 g butter
500 ml (2 cups) sugar
3 eggs
650 ml (just under 2⅔ cups) buttermilk

Preheat the oven to 180 °C. Place both flours, the baking powder, bran cereal, raisins and nuts in a bowl. Melt the butter in a saucepan, add the sugar and stir until dissolved. Set aside to cool. Beat the eggs, add the buttermilk and then add this to the melted butter and sugar Make a well in the centre of the dry ingredients and pour in the butter and buttermilk mixture. Mix well. Turn into greased loaf pans (15 x 30 cm) and bake in the oven for 40 minutes until done. Cool for at least 2 hours before cutting into rusk-sized pieces. Dry out in a warm oven (about 100 °C) for 4–6 hours, or overnight in the warming drawer on very low heat. Store in an airtight container. **MAKES 40–50**

The Tanqua-Karoo is an outpost of nature where man's intrusion is still but a light touch.

SKUINSKOEK (DIAGONAL COOKIES)

This is a traditional speciality of the Williston and Hantam areas of the Karoo.

250 g butter
2.5 kg white bread flour
750 ml (3 cups) sugar
3 x 10 g packets instant dried yeast
15 ml (1 Tbsp) salt
10 ml (2 tsp) ground ginger
10 ml (2 tsp) ground cinnamon
Grated lemon or naartjie peel
25 ml (5 tsp) aniseed
± 1.5 litres (± 6 cups) warm water
3 x 750 ml oil for deep-frying

SYRUP
500 ml (2 cups) sugar
750 ml (3 cups) water
5 ml (1 tsp) salt

Rub the butter into the flour. Add the rest of the ingredients, except the water and oil, and knead together with the warm water. Leave aside in a warm place to rise. Knock back and roll out on a board that has been sprayed to prevent the mixture sticking. Cut diagonal lines through the dough from left to right and do the same in the other direction to end up with 4 cm x 4 cm diamond-shaped pieces. Set aside to rise again.

Syrup: Boil all the syrup ingredients together for 5 minutes and then remove from the heat. Use when it is lukewarm.

Heat about 3 x 750 ml bottles of oil in a large cast-iron pot. Deep-fry the diamonds of dough and, when done, toss them in a brown paper bag with a little flour to get rid of excess oil. Place the diamonds in a sieve and pour the syrup over them until they become soft and shiny. This ensures a longer shelf life. **MAKES 30–40 DIAMONDS**

Note: Test the heat of the oil by tossing a match (with head removed) into it. If the oil has reached the correct temperature, tiny bubbles will form on both sides of the match. Pioneer housewives always added a peeled potato to the oil to keep it clean while the skuinskoek were frying.

VINEGAR FRUITCAKE

250 ml (1 cup) dried fruit cake mix
60 ml (¼ cup) sherry
30 ml (2 Tbsp) vinegar
5 ml (1 tsp) bicarbonate of soda
125 ml (½ cup) milk
250 ml (1 cup) sugar
10 ml (2 tsp) vanilla essence
2 eggs
750 ml (3 cups) cake flour
2.5 ml (½ tsp) salt
250 g butter, melted
Brown sugar, ground ginger and ground cinnamon to taste

Soak the cake mix in the sherry for a few hours.

Preheat the oven to 180 °C. Place the vinegar, bicarbonate of soda, milk, sugar, vanilla essence, eggs (one at a time), cake flour and salt into a mixing bowl, stirring lightly after each addition. Add the fruit and the sherry in which it was soaked. Beat well with an electric mixer for 5–7 minutes. Add the melted butter and stir well. Scoop into a greased loaf tin (12.5 cm x 24 cm) and sprinkle the top with a mixture of brown sugar, ginger and cinnamon. Bake in the oven for about 1½ hours until done. **MAKES 1 LOAF**

BRAN RUSKS

500 g butter
5 x 250 ml (5 cups) bran
500 ml (2 cups) sugar
250 ml (1 cup) fresh cream
500 ml (2 cups) buttermilk or milk (or a mixture of the two)
1 kg brown self-raising flour

Preheat the oven to 180 °C. Melt the butter and, while it is melting, mix the bran, sugar and cream together. Add the butter and buttermilk, then the self-raising flour and mix to form a soft dough. Press into a large well-greased pan or bake in 2–3 smaller bread pans. Bake in the oven for 30–45 minutes. Turn out carefully – this is important because these loaves break easily when they are hot so slide them out onto a cooling rack. Cool, cut up and dry out in a warm oven (about 100 °C) for 4–6 hours, or overnight in a warming drawer on very low heat.
MAKES 40–50

Bran Rusks

Pannekoek with Cinnamon Sugar

PANNEKOEK (PANCAKES)

30 ml (2 Tbsp) soft butter
375 ml (1½ cups) cake flour
5 ml (1 tsp) bicarbonate of soda
5 ml (1 tsp) baking powder
2.5 ml (½ tsp) salt
15 ml (1 Tbsp) sugar
3 eggs, separated
500 ml (2 cups) sour milk
Oil for frying
Cinnamon and sugar (optional)

Cream the butter and mix in the flour, bicarbonate of soda, baking powder, salt and sugar. Beat the egg yolks well, add the sour milk and continue beating. Add this to the flour mixture and beat well. Whisk the egg whites until they form soft peaks. Fold in. Set aside to rest for a while. Heat a little oil in a pan, pour in only sufficient batter to cover the bottom and leave until the mixture is brown and loosens underneath. Turn and brown the other side. Slide out onto a clean plate, cover and keep warm. Repeat until all the batter is used. Serve with a sweet or savoury filling or simply with cinnamon and sugar. **MAKES ABOUT 20**

MILK TART

6 eggs
500 ml (2 cups) sugar
30 ml (2 Tbsp) custard powder
30 ml (2 Tbsp) cornflour
30 ml (2 Tbsp) cake flour
Pinch of salt
2 litres (8 cups) milk
15 ml (1 Tbsp) butter
2 x quantity cold water pastry (see page 68)
Ground cinnamon and sugar for dusting

Preheat the oven to 180 °C. Separate 2 eggs and whisk the whites until stiff. Gradually add 250 ml (1 cup) sugar, beating all the while until the sugar has dissolved and it reaches a meringue stage. In a separate bowl, beat the rest of the eggs and the 2 yolks with the rest of the sugar. Add the custard powder, cornflour, cake flour and salt. Add 250 ml (1 cup) milk. Place the rest of the milk in a saucepan with the butter and bring to the boil. Remove from the heat. Add the cold milk mixture, stirring all the time. Then fold in the meringue. Line six pie dishes with the cold water pastry, ensuring that the bottom layer is very thin. Pour the filling into the pastry shells and bake at in the oven for 20 minutes until the mixture has almost set. (The mixture will set on standing.) Cool and sprinkle with cinnamon and sugar. **MAKES 6 X 23 CM TARTS**

NECTARINE PIE

1 egg
125 ml (½ cup) sugar
60 ml (4 Tbsp) cake flour
225 ml (just under 1 cup) fresh cream
5 ml (1 tsp) ground cinnamon
1 ml (¼ tsp) almond essence
5 or 6 ripe, firm nectarines
1 x 22 cm unbaked pie shell

Preheat the oven to 180 °C. Bring a large pot of water to the boil. Beat the egg and sugar together. Add the flour, cream, cinnamon and essence. Set aside. Place the nectarines into the boiling water for 30–45 seconds. Using a slotted spoon, remove them and place under cold running water. Skin, cut in half and remove the pips. Place the halves onto the pie shell, cut side down. (You can also cut the nectarines into slices and arrange these neatly on top of the pie shell.) Pour over the cream mixture and bake for 35–40 minutes until set. Serve hot or cold with whipped cream. **SERVES 6–8**

KOEKSISTERS

1.25 kg (9 cups) flour
7.5 ml (1½ tsp) salt
125 g butter
45 ml (3 Tbsp) baking powder
3 eggs
500 ml (2 cups) milk
500 ml (2 cups) water

SYRUP
1.25 kg sugar
2 litres (8 cups) water
5 ml (1 tsp) cream of tartar

Sift the flour and salt together. Rub in the butter and then add the baking powder. Beat the eggs. Mix the beaten eggs with 250 ml (1 cup) milk and 250 ml (1 cup) water and slowly add this liquid to the dry ingredients. Add just enough of the remaining liquid, mixing all the time, until a firm dough is formed. (The dough must not be too sloppy, nor too stiff.) Knead well. Roll out to about 1 cm thick and then cut into short strips. Plait the strips and place on a greased baking sheet to rest for 15 minutes. Keep the dough covered so that it doesn't dry out.

Syrup: Place the sugar and water in a saucepan. Heat slowly so that the sugar can dissolve. Add the cream of tartar just as the syrup begins to boil. Boil for 7 minutes. Cool and refrigerate.

To finish: Heat 3–4 x 750 ml bottles of oil in a deep pan. Put batches of koeksisters into a frying basket and deep-fry until golden. Remove, drain and immediately drop the koeksisters into the ice-cold syrup. Remove with a slotted spoon and drain on a cooling rack. **MAKES ABOUT 10 DOZEN (120)**

Note: Take care not to undercook or get doughy bits in the plaits. The final product – which is best served cold – should be almost translucent, as fragile as glass, yet crunchy and dripping with delicious syrup. No-one knows how these delicacies acquired their name. In *Land of the Afternoon*, Lawrence Green states that one day a mother was preparing these when her little daughter asked what she was making. Her reply was 'Koek, sustertjie' (Cake, little sister) and this seems to have stuck.

GREEN FIG TART

1 packet Tennis or Marie biscuits, crushed
60 ml (¼ cup) melted butter

FILLING
10 ml (2 tsp) gelatine powder
30 ml (2 Tbsp) cold water
1 x 380 g can evaporated milk
175 ml (just over ⅔ cup) sugar
3 eggs, separated
250 ml (1 cup) finely sliced preserved green figs
125 ml (½ cup) chopped nuts of choice,
e.g. walnuts or pecans
12 red glacé cherries, quartered
2.5 ml (½ tsp) almond essence
125 ml (½ cup) fresh cream, whipped
2 additional preserved figs, cut into thin slices

Make a base by mixing together the crushed biscuits and melted butter. Press into a pie plate.

Filling: Soak the gelatine in the cold water. Heat the evaporated milk in a double boiler. Beat half the sugar and the eggs yolks together, stir in a little of the hot milk and then add this mixture to the rest of the milk in the double boiler. Continue heating, stirring continuously, until the mixture thickens. Remove from the heat and stir in the gelatine, figs, nuts, cherries and almond essence. Whisk the egg whites and remaining sugar until stiff peaks form and fold this into the milk mixture. Pour over the biscuit base and refrigerate. Before serving, beat the cream until stiff, and spread over the tart. Decorate with slices of preserved fig. **SERVES 6–8**

VERSATILE FLOP-PROOF LAYER CAKE

In two sizes (23 cm layer pan or large oven pan)

3 eggs	4 eggs
375 ml (1½ cups) sugar	440 ml (1¾ cups) sugar
Pinch of salt	Pinch of salt
5 ml (1 tsp) vanilla essence	10 ml (2 tsp) vanilla essence
250 g butter	375 g butter
250 ml (1 cup) milk	500 ml (2 cups) milk
500 ml (2 cups) cake flour	750 ml (3 cups) cake flour
20 ml (4 tsp) baking powder	30 ml (2 Tbsp) baking powder

Preheat the oven to 180 °C. Beat the eggs and sugar well until they turn white. Add the salt and vanilla essence. Heat the butter and milk in a saucepan, just until the butter has melted. Sift the flour and baking powder, and then add the egg mixture. Stir well. Add the melted butter and milk. Bake in two 23 cm greased layer tins (or if making the large version in a large oven pan) in the oven for 20 minutes. **SERVES 6–8 (OR 16 IF USING THE OVEN PAN)**

Koeksisters

The Karoo's a 'sweet tooth' haven

The Karoo's the ideal place for anyone with a sweet tooth. Henry Lichtenstein said that European gourmands would scarcely envy anything as much as the desserts served at the end of a meal in this area. Fresh and preserved fruits are still part of the Karoo, but here one also finds good hearty traditional puddings, home-made sweets, old-fashioned cool drinks and lemonades. Among the best places to discover most of these traditional delights are 'pudding stalls' at small town church bazaars. *Village Life* editor, Annalize Mouton, was once horrified to read that dessert was originally regarded as food to be served after the table had been cleared – or deserted – of everything, even the cloth! 'We would never dream of treating traditional South African puddings with such contempt,' she exclaimed.

Choose a route – drive to De Aar, once a bustling railway junction, or to Deelfontein, the largest surgical and convalescent hospital set up by the British Army during the Anglo-Boer War.

Desserts and
Other Delights

Deelfontein

Desserts

QUINCE CRUMBLE

125 g butter
150 ml (just under ⅔ cup) sugar
250 ml (1 cup) self-raising flour
1 x 1-litre bottle preserved quinces
125 ml (½ cup) chopped walnuts

Preheat the oven to 180 °C. Rub the butter, sugar and flour together until a fine crumble forms. Drain the quinces. Grease a 20 cm pie plate and sprinkle half the crumbs onto the bottom of the plate. Arrange the quinces on top of the crumble. Mix the walnuts with the rest of the crumble and sprinkle over the fruit. Bake in the oven for about 20 minutes until golden and crispy. Serve with custard and thick cream. **SERVES 6–8**

Note: This crumble is also delicious made with canned apples, pears, apricots or plums.

STEWED QUINCES

250 ml (1 cup) sugar
500 ml (2 cups) water
Juice of ½ lemon
1 kg quinces, peeled, pitted and cut into chunks
Custard powder for thickening

Dissolve the sugar in the water and lemon juice in a saucepan. Bring to the boil. Add the quince chunks and simmer for 20–25 minutes until the quinces are soft. Thicken slightly with a little custard powder. Serve hot. **SERVES 4–6**

Note: This is also delicious as a filling for a flan or as a side dish with venison.

APRICOT PUDDING

60 ml (4 Tbsp) butter
60 ml (4 Tbsp) sugar
4 eggs
125 ml (½ cup) cake flour
5 ml (1 tsp) bicarbonate of soda dissolved in a little milk
75 ml (5 Tbsp) apricot jam

SYRUP
250 ml (1 cup) sugar
1.25 litres (5 cups) milk
250 ml (1 cup) fresh cream

Cream the butter and sugar together. Add the eggs, one at a time, beating well after each addition. Add the flour, bicarbonate of soda and jam. Set aside while you make the syrup.

Syrup: Preheat the oven to 180 °C. Place the sugar in a saucepan and scald lightly until slightly caramelized. Take care not to let it burn. Slowly add the milk and stir to dissolve the sugar. Add the cream. Pour the syrup into a deep ovenproof dish and spoon the dough into this. Bake for about 30 minutes until the pudding is cooked and the sauce has thickened. **SERVES 4–6**

Quince Crumble

Delicious Kluitjies

DELICIOUS KLUITJIES (SWEET DUMPLINGS)

250 ml (1 cup) cake flour
10 ml (2 tsp) baking powder
Pinch of salt
10 ml (2 tsp) butter
2 eggs
Dash of milk
Ground cinnamon and sugar for sprinkling

SAUCE
250 ml (1 cup) water (use some of the water from the pot in which the kluitjies were cooked)
125 ml (½ cup) sugar
12.5 ml (2½ tsp) cornflour
Pinch of salt
25 ml (5 tsp) butter

Place a saucepan of water on the stove to boil. Place the flour, baking powder and salt in a bowl and, using fingertips, lightly rub in the butter. Beat eggs with a little milk and add to the mixture. Spoon small amounts of the dough (about 5 ml (1 tsp) measures and not more than four at a time) into the boiling water. Place the lid on the pot and, after 5 minutes, turn the *kluitjies* (dumplings) to cook the other side. When done, lift them from the boiling water using a slotted spoon and drain. Place in a shallow dish. Sprinkle with cinnamon and sugar and dot with butter. Continue until the entire mixture is used up.

Sauce: Mix all the sauce ingredients together in a saucepan. Bring to the boil and simmer until slightly thickened. Pour over the kluitjies. **SERVES 4–6**

MILK KLUITJIES (MILK DUMPLINGS)

30 ml (2 Tbsp) cornflour (add a little sugar to taste)
1 litre (4 cups) milk
2 eggs, separated
Pinch of salt
25 ml (5 tsp) baking powder
Ground cinnamon and sugar for sprinkling
Butter

Mix the cornflour to a paste with a little of the cold milk. Beat the egg yolks well and add to the rest of the milk. Add salt. Heat this mixture in a saucepan, stirring to ensure that it does not curdle. Add the cornflour mixture and cook until the mixture thickens. Whisk the egg whites until stiff peaks form. Fold in the baking powder and fold this into the milk mixture. Heat again. Scoop spoonfuls into a shallow bowl and sprinkle with cinnamon sugar. Dot with butter. **SERVES 4–6**

Note: This pudding can be varied by adding leftover cooked rice to the mixture.

CITRUS BAKED CUSTARD WITH BRÛLÉE TOPPING

500 ml (2 cups) milk
125 ml (½ cup) sugar
Peel of 1 orange and 1 lemon (remove all the pith to prevent the mixture becoming bitter)
1 cinnamon stick
2 eggs plus 2 egg yolks
60 ml (4 Tbsp) crushed biscuit crumbs (Marie or Tennis)
Pinch of salt
Ground cinnamon for topping
Castor sugar for brûlée topping

Pour the milk into a saucepan and add the sugar, peels and cinnamon stick. Bring to the boil. Remove from the heat and leave to infuse (draw) for about 30 minutes. Strain. Preheat the oven to 150 °C. Beat the eggs and add to the strained milk mixture. Add the biscuit crumbs and salt. Pour into a 1 litre greased ovenproof bowl, sprinkle with ground cinnamon and bake in a pan of hot water in the oven for about 45 minutes, or until set and golden on top. Remove from the oven and cool.

Note: The flavour is enhanced if this pudding is made the day before.

Brûlée topping: Before serving sprinkle about 3 mm of castor sugar all over the top of the pudding. Then, place it under the grill and leave until the sugar becomes caramel coloured. Take care that it does not burn. Remove and cool. The pudding will then be covered with what looks like a thin layer of caramel-coloured glass. Serve with whipped cream or ice cream. **SERVES 4–6**

ORANGE PUDDING

SYRUP
1.25 litres (5 cups) water
500 ml (2 cups) sugar
10 ml (2 tsp) ground cinnamon
2 oranges, finely chopped (peel and all)

PUDDING MIXTURE
10 ml (2 tsp) baking powder dissolved in a little vinegar
500 ml (2 cups) finely chopped pitted dates
250 ml (1 cup) warm milk
30 ml (2 Tbsp) butter or margarine
15 ml (1 Tbsp) golden syrup
500 ml (2 cups) cake flour
5 ml (1 tsp) salt

Syrup: Place all the sauce ingredients in a large saucepan and bring to the boil.

Pudding: Dissolve the baking powder in a little vinegar and pour over the dates. Then, pour the warm milk over the dates. Set aside to cool. Mix the rest of the ingredients together and add to the date mixture. Spoon the date mixture into the syrup in the saucepan, cover with a lid. Bring to the boil and then simmer for 1 hour. Insert a skewer into the centre – if it comes out clean the pudding is done. Scoop into serving dishes and serve with custard or whipped cream. **SERVES 6–8**

Note: It is important to use a large saucepan when making this pudding because the mixture boils over very easily.

FRESH RHUBARB BREAD PUDDING

8 slices white bread, crusts removed,
toasted and cubed
60 ml (4 Tbsp) butter
375 ml (1½ cups) milk
5 eggs
300 ml (1¼ cups) white sugar
5 ml (1 tsp) ground cinnamon
Salt to taste
500 ml (2 cups) washed and diced
rhubarb stalks
60 ml (¼ cup) chopped walnuts

Preheat the oven to 160 °C. Place the bread cubes in a buttered casserole dish. Heat the butter and milk in a saucepan and bring to boiling point (but do not boil). Pour the hot milk mixture over the bread cubes and leave this to stand for 5 minutes. In a glass bowl, whisk together the eggs and sugar. Add the cinnamon and salt. Stir in the rhubarb. Pour this over the bread mixture and stir gently to blend evenly. Sprinkle the walnuts on top and bake for 50 minutes in the oven until nicely browned on top. Leave to stand for 10 minutes before serving. **SERVES 6–8**

Citrus Baked Custard with Brûlée Topping

Decadent Ice Cream

DECADENT ICE CREAM

1 x 380 g can evaporated milk, chilled overnight
250 ml (1 cup) castor sugar
500 ml (2 cups) thick fresh farm cream, chilled overnight
10 ml (2 tsp) vanilla essence

Beat the evaporated milk well. Slowly add the castor sugar. Whip the cream until stiff, and then add it to the evaporated milk mixture. Beat again and, while beating, add vanilla essence. Pour into a bowl. Cover with clingfilm and freeze until required. **SERVES 6–8**

SKURWEPADDA (SPICY VINEGAR PUDDING)

500 ml (2 cups) cake flour
10 ml (2 tsp) bicarbonate of soda
Pinch of salt
30 ml (2 Tbsp) butter
125–190 ml (½–¾ cup) milk
30 ml (2 Tbsp) apricot jam (or a bit more if desired)

SYRUP
250 ml (1 cup) water
2.5 ml (½ tsp) ground ginger
15 ml (1 Tbsp) ground cinnamon
2.5 ml (½ tsp) salt
250 ml (1 cup) yellow sugar
125 ml (½ cup) vinegar

Place the flour, bicarbonate of soda and salt in a bowl. Rub in the butter and then mix to a dough with the milk. Stir in the apricot jam.

Syrup: Place all the sauce ingredients in a saucepan and bring to the boil. Add tablespoonfuls of dough to the boiling liquid and boil rapidly for 5 minutes. Reduce the heat and simmer gently for 1 hour. Serve with custard. **SERVES 4–6**

Many dams are hidden in the hills in this arid zone.

SAMP PUDDING

10 ml (2 tsp) butter
125 ml (½ cup) sugar (or more if desired)
4 eggs (2 separated)
500 ml (2 cups) cooked samp
750 ml (3 cups) boiling milk
Grated nutmeg

Preheat the oven to 180 °C. Beat the butter and sugar together. Add the 2 whole eggs, one at a time, and beat well after each addition. Add the 2 egg yolks, the samp and boiling milk. Spoon the mixture into an ovenproof dish. Whisk the egg whites until peaks form, and then add a little sugar. Spread over the samp mixture and grate a little nutmeg on top. Place in the oven until the meringue topping has cooked through. **SERVES 4–6**

Note: This recipe was a favourite of the late Tannie Anna Esterhuizen and her sister Tullie, who in the early 1930s ran Williston's first maternity home. In those days the small Karoo towns each had their own power stations to supply electricity, but these switched off at 21h00. However, in Williston, if anyone went into labour at night, the power station staff were called out and their machinery was started up again so that there would be sufficient light for the baby to be delivered. Of course, in such a little town everyone knew whose baby was due. The moment they heard the power station starting up again they were well aware that there would soon be a new member of their community. Next morning many townsfolk arrived to welcome the infant with flowers, jackets and bootees. Anna traditionally made this delicious pudding to serve to new mothers.

OLD-FASHIONED SNOW PUDDING

1 litre (4 cups) water
375 ml (1½ cups) sugar
Pinch of salt
45 ml (3 Tbsp) cornflour
3 egg whites, stiffly beaten
2.5–5 ml (½–1 tsp) tartaric acid
5 ml (1 tsp) lemon essence

Bring the water, sugar and salt to the boil in a saucepan. Mix the cornflour to a paste with a little water and add to the boiling sugar water. Remove from the heat and fold in the stiffly beaten egg whites, tartaric acid and lemon essence. Pour into a bowl and leave to cool. **SERVES 4–6**

Karnmelk Poeding (Buttermilk Pudding)

This traditional and amusing old recipe for buttermilk pudding comes out of Maxie Hugo's grandmother's recipe book. Maxie was intrigued because the measures were given by the 'glass' and not 'cup'. The recipe also refers to karnmelk and not karingmelk, as buttermilk is known today. Also, there is no indication of spoon size, or oven temperature, but Maxie does remember this pudding was a family favourite. (1 glass = ± 300 ml)

1 glas soet melk (1 glass sweet milk)
1 glas karnmelk (1 glass buttermilk)
1 glas suiker (1 glass sugar)

2 eiers (2 eggs)
2 lepels meel (2 spoons flour)

Eers die suiker en geel van eiers en meel moet aangemaak word met 'n bietjie van die soet melk, dan die karnmelk en laaste die wit van eiers. Bak.
(First the sugar and egg yolks should be mixed with a little sweet milk. Lastly add the buttermilk and egg whites. Bake.)

QUINCE TART WITH CREAM SAUCE

37.5 ml (2½ Tbsp) butter
150 ml (just under ⅔ cup) sugar
3 eggs
250 ml (1 cup) cake flour
1 ml (¼ tsp) salt
5 ml (1 tsp) baking powder
125 ml (½ cup) milk
1 x 500 ml jar preserved quinces

CREAM SAUCE
250 ml (1 cup) sugar
250 ml (1 cup) fresh cream
2.5 ml (½ tsp) caramel essence

Preheat the oven to 180 °C. Cream the butter and sugar. Add the eggs, one by one, beating well after each addition. Sift the dry ingredients together and add to the mixture alternately with the milk. Mix well. Scoop the mixture into a greased baking dish (25 x 30 cm). Drain the quinces and cut into small pieces. Spread these evenly across the top of the dough and bake in the oven for 45 minutes.

Cream sauce: Place all the sauce ingredients into a saucepan. Stir and bring to the boil. Simmer gently for 5 minutes and pour over the quince tart as soon as it comes out of the oven. Serve hot or cold with whipped cream. **SERVES 8–10**

Small clumps of blue gum trees dot the Karoo, signalling habitation like this little cottage on the R64 near Montagu.

Pomegranate Dessert

POMEGRANATE DESSERT

6–8 pomegranates
125 ml (½ cup) sugar
125 ml (½ cup) schnapps

Shell the pomegranates, removing all the flesh. Place the fruit in a flat glass bowl. Mix the sugar and schnapps together and pour over the fruit. Chill very well and serve with thick cream or ice cream. **SERVES 4–6**

Note: The amount of schnapps and sugar depends on the amount of fruit, but always ensure that equal quantities of both are used. It doesn't matter if the sugar doesn't totally dissolve at first, it will dissolve on the fruit. These days pomegranates are not too easy to find, but in bygone days pomegranate hedges were a feature of the Karoo. Pomegranates are a rich source of vital nutrients and contain almost three times as many anti-oxidant vitamins as red wine or green tea.

TRADITIONAL BUTTERMILK PUDDING

15 ml (1 Tbsp) butter
3 eggs
190 ml (¾ cup) white sugar
125 ml (½ cup) self-raising flour
500 ml (2 cups) buttermilk
250 ml (1 cup) milk
2.5 ml (½ tsp) salt

Preheat the oven to 180 °C. Melt the butter in a 2-litre volume ovenproof dish. Break the eggs into a mixing bowl, add the sugar and beat well. Add the flour, buttermilk and milk alternately. Stir in the salt. Pour the mixture over the melted butter in the ovenproof dish and bake for about 40 minutes until the pudding has set and the top is light brown. Serve warm. **SERVES 4–6**

OUMA'S SAGO PUDDING

250 ml (1 cup) sago
1 litre (4 cups) milk
Salt to taste
5 eggs, separated
125 ml (½ cup) sugar
5 ml (1 tsp) vanilla essence
75 ml (5 Tbsp) smooth apricot jam
65 g butter
Ground cinnamon

The day before: Soak the sago in water overnight.

Next day: Drain the sago. Preheat the oven to 160 °C. Bring the milk to the boil in a saucepan. Add the sago and salt and simmer until cooked (the sago becomes translucent). Beat the egg yolks with the sugar and add. Simmer for a minute or two. Remove from the heat. Whisk the egg whites until they form soft peaks, and then fold into the mixture. Add vanilla essence. Pour half the mixture into a greased ovenproof dish and gently spread with a layer of apricot jam. Pour over the rest of the mixture. Dot with butter, sprinkle with cinnamon and bake in the oven for 30–45 minutes until golden brown on top. **SERVES 4–6**

Beverages

GRAN'S GINGER BEER

9 litres cold water
100 g whole ginger, bruised
10 ml (2 tsp) instant dried yeast
15 ml (1 Tbsp) citric or tartaric acid
6 x 250 ml (6 cups total) sugar

Mix all the ingredients together and leave to stand for 24 hours. Strain and bottle. Chill very well to prevent too much gas forming (if this happens the bottles may explode). Serve chilled. **MAKES ABOUT 14 X 750 ML BOTTLES**

Gran's Ginger Beer

QUICK AND EASY TRADITIONAL GINGER BEER

6 litres cold water
5 x 250 ml (5 cups total) sugar
37.5 ml (2½ Tbsp) instant dried yeast
60 ml (4 Tbsp) ground ginger
45 ml (3 Tbsp) cream of tartar
60 ml (4 Tbsp) raisins, with seeds

Mix all the ingredients together and leave to stand overnight.

Next day: Strain through a muslin cloth, and then bottle and cork. Leave to stand for 2 days before refrigerating and using. **MAKES ABOUT 10 X 750 ML BOTTLES**

QUINCE COOL DRINK SYRUP

24 x 250 ml (24 cups total) liquid in which quinces have been cooked
12 x 250 ml (12 cups total) sugar
2 x 25 g packets tartaric acid

Mix all the ingredients together and heat to boiling point. Pour into sterilized bottles. Dilute the syrup with water to taste for drinking. This also makes a delicious ice-cream syrup and pudding sauce. **MAKES ABOUT 8 X 750 ML BOTTLES OF CONCENTRATED SYRUP**

LEMON SYRUP

2.5 litres (10 cups) water
500 ml (2 cups) freshly squeezed lemon juice
Grated peel of 8 lemons
4 x 500 ml (8 cups total) sugar
15 ml (1 Tbsp) tartaric acid
15 ml (1 Tbsp) Epsom salts

Bring the water to the boil. Place the other ingredients in a bowl. Pour the boiling water over the ingredients. Stir well to ensure everything is well mixed and dissolved. Leave to stand overnight. Bottle. **MAKES ABOUT 6 X 750 ML BOTTLES**

Note: This is a concentrated syrup and needs to be diluted with water before serving.

PRICKLY PEAR SYRUP

5 kg red prickly pears
2 litres (8 cups) water
350 ml (just under 1½ cups) lemon juice
2.5 kg sugar
15 ml (1 Tbsp) tartaric acid
15 ml (1 Tbsp) citric acid
15 ml (1 Tbsp) Epsom salts
2.5 ml (½ tsp) salt

Peel the prickly pears and boil in the water until tender. Strain and rub the pulp through a sieve to remove the pips. Use 1.5 litres (6 cups) of this mixture and add to the rest of the ingredients. Stir well to ensure all ingredients have dissolved. Bottle. **MAKES 6 X 750 ML BOTTLES OF CONCENTRATED SYRUP**

Note: This is a concentrate and should be diluted with water before serving. It also makes a delicious ice-cream sauce and can be used to pour over milk puddings, such as melkkos or milk tart.

Preserves

Store summer on the pantry shelf

Pioneer farmers planted orchards, vineyards and vegetable gardens as soon as they arrived in the Karoo. Travellers of the *wapad* (wagon route) often commented on these and the fact that many fruit trees were grown from pips. By 1797 Abraham le Clerq's farm Hooyvlakte (present-day Beaufort West) produced such a quantity of dried fruit, raisins, wine and brandy that he took wagonloads back to the Cape to sell. At times his wife did this long trip on her own, with only the *touleier* (leader of the oxen) for company. A Ceres farmer, Van der Merwe, discovered that snow on the Gydo Pass made the area ideal for cherry production, so he planted huge orchards of Californian black cherries. In 1803 Augusta de Mist mentions a Bokkeveld valley covered with orange, citron, fig, apricot and cherry trees. Fruit was produced in this area on a small scale until about 1900, when the industry mushroomed. Today Ceres, one of South Africa's largest fruit and vegetable producing areas, is internationally famous – a far cry from the days when pioneer exporters travelled from farm to farm personally packing and shipping grapes, peaches and pears. In 1862 Daisy Junius wrote of mulberry, sweet orange, lemon and pomegranate trees heavy with fruit on the winding road to Prince Albert. Today the area is well known for figs and nectarines, while export apricots have put Laingsburg on the map. When Beaufort West was established, by-laws were passed making the planting of fruit trees mandatory and every dwelling was graced by mulberry, peach, pear, orange and lemon trees. Farms in the district also had large orchards. Overwhelmed by the aroma H A L Hamelberg named it 'the land where the citrus blooms'. Delicious grapes led to Klaarstroom being hailed as the 'Constantia' of the Karoo, and a vine planted by Rev. Charles Murray at Reinet House in Graaff-Reinet grew to rival its counterpart at Hampton Court, England. Pear trees still grace streets in Beaufort West and Loxton. And Murraysburg made it into the record books with the longest quince hedge in the world. Today preserved quinces, the ideal accompaniment to mutton and venison dishes, remain a taste treat in the Karoo.

Home-made Mustard

30–100 ml (2 Tbsp–a bit under ½ cup) strong mustard powder (depending on the strength desired)
190 ml (¾ cup) sugar, or to taste
10 ml (2 tsp) cake flour
1 ml (¼ tsp) salt, or to taste
4 eggs, beaten
250 ml (1 cup) vinegar (white vinegar only can be used or a mixture of half white and half brown)

Mix the mustard powder, sugar, flour and salt together. Add the beaten eggs and mix well. Add the vinegar, beating well all the time to prevent the mixture from curdling. Place in a double boiler or in a glass bowl over boiling water and cook for 10–15 minutes, stirring all the time to prevent lumps forming. Cool and bottle. Cover and store in the refrigerator for up to 1 month. **MAKES 500 ML (2 CUPS)**

Olive Paste

350 g black or green olives, pitted and chopped
4 large cloves garlic, crushed
100 g capers
1 x 45 g can anchovy fillets
15 ml (1 Tbsp) lemon juice
15 ml (1 Tbsp) brandy
10 ml (2 tsp) good quality olive oil
Salt and freshly ground black pepper to taste

Using a mortar and pestle, pound and rub all the ingredients together until a smooth paste is formed. Scoop into a jar and refrigerate. Leave to stand for 24 hours for flavours to develop. Serve on slivers of toast or with cheese as a snack with drinks. Will keep in the refrigerator for about a month. **MAKES 500 ML (2 CUPS)**

Olive Paste

Lemon Curd

Fruit

LEMON CURD

Juice of 10 lemons (± 500 ml)
Grated peel of 2 lemons (optional)
1 kg sugar
8 eggs
250 g butter

Put all the ingredients into a double boiler and stir continuously for 20 minutes until the mixture thickens. Bottle while hot. Spread over jam or toast or use as a filling for tarts and puddings and between the layers of sandwich cakes.
MAKES 4 X 450 G BOTTLES

Note: Some people don't like the texture if lemon rind is added.

RUMPOT

This is made in fruit season to ensure that all the little bits of fruit – bits of marked fruit, hail-damaged fruit, and the bits of fruit that do not fit into the preserving jars – are used. Use an earthenware jar with a well-fitting cork lid. Place a layer of fruit on the bottom of the pot. Hard fruit, such as apples, must first be pricked. Sprinkle a layer of sugar over the fruit and cover with rum. Seal the pot. Continue adding fruit, sugar and rum, sealing the pot well after each addition, until the end of the season. Then, seal the pot and store for at least three months. The rum can then be served as an excellent fruit liqueur and the fruit eaten with buttermilk pudding, or milk *snysels* (dough threads).

GREEN FIG PRESERVE

Figs for whole green fig preserve are ready for picking from the middle of October. Boil until soft. Remove immediately from the boiling water and place in cold water. Scrape off any marks and cut a cross into the bottom of each fig. In a large bucket, mix 25 ml (5 tsp) slaked lime with 5 litres water. Place the figs in this mixture overnight.

The next day, prepare a syrup using 750 ml (3 cups) water to each 250 ml (1 cup) sugar. Flavour with whole cloves or ginger as desired. Rinse the figs well and boil small batches in the syrup until they are shiny. Bottle. These can be served with fresh bread and butter, as a dessert with ice cream, cream or custard and chopped or sliced for use in tarts and cakes. Preserved green figs are also delicious with cold meats, or as a starter, cut in quarters and threaded onto toothpicks with cheese.

Note: In the old traditional recipe 7 lb (3.1 kg) sugar was recommended for each 5 lb (2.2 kg) figs.

BOTTLED APRICOTS

Choose firm, just-ripe apricots (1–1.5 kg). Wash well. Do not peel or halve. Make a heavy syrup from 200 ml (¾ cup) sugar to 250 ml (1 cup) water. Heat slowly until the sugar dissolves, and then bring to the boil. Place the whole apricots in this syrup and boil rapidly until just cooked, but not soft. Place the fruit carefully into sterilized bottles, cover with hot syrup and seal. Leave for a few months before serving.

Note: These apricots are delicious as dessert or for serving with meat. They have a delicious almond aroma and flavour. The syrup also has this flavour and makes an excellent sauce for baked puddings, or for simply pouring over ice cream.

PRESERVED 'SOFT' PEACHES

Few people think of preserving early or soft peaches
– these are the loose-pipped 'white peaches' and
are quite delicious preserved and served this way
– but this is easy to do and rewarding because after
standing in their jars for a while the syrup turns a
delightful shade of pale pink. Choose just ripened
peaches. Pull the skins off, halve and remove the
pips. Prick each half with a darning needle in several
places and lay the halves in a preserving pan. Cover
with sugar – use 2.5 kg for each 4 kg of fruit. Leave to
stand overnight. Next day, heat gently until the sugar
dissolves, and then boil rapidly until the juice thickens
slightly and the fruit softens. Take care not to let the
peach halves get too soft or they will lose their shape.
Bottle in sterilized jars. These are delicious served
with cream or ice cream as a pudding or for a flan
filling or even for a topping.

ORANGE PRESERVE

Cut each whole orange into quarters or slices. For
each 500 g fruit add 750 ml (3 cups) water and leave
to soak overnight. Next morning, boil until soft in the
same water in which the fruit was soaked. Leave to
stand for 12 hours. Add equal quantities of sugar to
fruit and boil until thick. Pour into sterilized bottles
while hot and seal.

Note: Ruby grapefruit can also be used for this recipe.

WATERMELON KONFYT
(PRESERVE)

The following mix is ideal for about 130 pieces of fruit

The day before: Peel and cut watermelon into
cubes. Prick well on all sides with a sharp fork. Soak
overnight in a lime solution made by dissolving
22.5 ml (1½ Tbsp) slaked lime in 3.5 litres water. Make
sure that all the pieces are fully submerged.

Next day: Drain and rinse. Boil the pieces in clean
water for approximately 15 minutes, then drain. Make
a syrup using 5 kg sugar to 5 litres water. Add the
pieces and boil for about 3 hours until the syrup has
thickened and cooked through the pieces. Carefully
place the pieces into sterilized bottles while hot,
cover with syrup and seal immediately.

Note: A watermelon once almost defeated an Irish
priest in the outlying hinterland. In the 1860s Rev.
James O'Haire had to visit some parishioners in an
isolated area. They were poor, so he thought he'd
take them some food. He settled on a watermelon
'as large as a good-sized bucket'. However, carrying
this 'monster' on his long journey by foot almost
overwhelmed him. He walked along, clutching the
melon to his chest while trying to hold his sunshade
above his head. The day was scorchingly hot and
perspiration 'poured down to my very boots'. Hungry
and exhausted, he stumbled on until he caught his
foot and fell. Totally overcome by fatigue, he sat on
a broken tree stump and 'cried bitterly', all the time
holding onto the melon. It had cracked and its water
trickled out onto his dusty robes. In time he gathered
his courage and proceeded, at last arriving at the
cottage 'a sorry sight and dog tired'. He drank a cup
of tea and went immediately to bed. As he was about
to doze off his hostess came in, bringing him a bowl
filled with watermelon slices.

PICKLED PEACHES

2–3 kg yellow cling peaches, washed
(do not peel)
1 whole clove for each peach half

Using a sharp knife, cut each peach in half, remove the pip and carefully insert a clove into the centre of the cavity left by the pip.

SYRUP
500 ml (2 cups) water
250 ml (1 cup) sugar
90 ml (6 Tbsp) vinegar
4 cinnamon sticks

Syrup: Place all the ingredients for the syrup into a saucepan and heat gently to allow the sugar to dissolve. Bring to the boil. Add the peaches in small batches and boil until soft. Carefully layer into bottles. Cover with syrup and seal while hot. **MAKES ABOUT 6 LARGE PRESERVING JARS (THE OLD 1 LB CONSOL JAR)**

QUINCE JELLY

1.5 kg (about 5) firm ripe quinces
1.5 litres (6 cups) water
1 kg sugar

Wash the quinces and cut them into chunks (do not peel and do not remove the pips). Put the quince chunks into a large saucepan with the water and bring to the boil. Simmer for 30–35 minutes until the fruit is soft. Then, strain the liquid from the quinces through a muslin jelly bag, or a colander lined with several thick layers of cheesecloth, into a glass bowl. Allow the liquid to drip through into the bowl undisturbed and overnight if necessary. Do not squeeze or press the pulp in any way as this will make the jelly cloudy. Once all the liquid has dripped through the bag, discard the pulp and pips. Then, using a 250 ml measuring cup, measure the juice into a clean saucepan. For every 500 ml (2 cups) of juice, add 250 ml (1 cup) of sugar. Slowly bring the liquid to the boil. Stir all the time to ensure that all the sugar dissolves before the liquid begins to boil. Boil rapidly and skim if necessary. The jelly is ready for bottling when a few drops of the liquid set and 'gel' as they cool on a chilled plate. Once this happens, pour the liquid into clean, warm, sterilized jars and seal while hot. When cold, this jelly has a rich pink colour and it is totally translucent. **MAKES ABOUT 750 ML**

Note: Apple jelly can be made in exactly the same way by using good tart cooking apples. A delicious jelly can also be made using a mixture of quinces and apples.

The mountains of the Karoo hide secluded valleys to delight hikers.

Onion Preserve

Vegetables

Onion Preserve

30 ml (2 Tbsp) sultanas
30 ml (2 Tbsp) sherry
100 g butter
3 large onions, thinly sliced into rings
60 ml (4 Tbsp) brown sugar
125 ml (½ cup) apple cider vinegar
15 ml (1 Tbsp) mustard seeds
2.5 cm piece fresh ginger, peeled and grated
Salt and freshly ground black pepper to taste

Place the sultanas and sherry in a glass bowl and soak for a few hours. Heat the butter in a heavy-bottomed saucepan and, stirring constantly, sauté the onions until they become translucent and the moisture from the butter evaporates. Add the sultanas and the sherry in which they soaked, the sugar and vinegar and bring the mixture to the boil. Simmer until the mixture thickens. Add the mustard seeds, ginger, salt and pepper. Bottle and store in the refrigerator. **MAKES ABOUT 250 ML (1 CUP)**

Note: This onion preserve keeps well in the refrigerator for about a month. It is an excellent accompaniment to cold meats and cheese platters.

Green Pepper Chutney

1 kg green peppers, cored, de-seeded and chopped
500 g onions, finely chopped
30 ml (2 Tbsp) olive oil
1 kg ripe tomatoes, skinned and chopped
2 cloves garlic, chopped
5 ml (1 tsp) ground ginger
5 ml (1 tsp) mixed spice
500 g sugar
250 ml (1 cup) sultanas
500 ml (2 cups) wine vinegar

Sauté the peppers and onions in oil for a few minutes to allow the volatile oils to escape. Leave this mixture to stand for a short while so that flavours can develop. Then, add all the other ingredients and cook gently until the mixture thickens. Take care not to let it burn. Bottle and store. This keeps very well for two or three months. **MAKES 2 X 500 ML JARS**

Green Pepper Jelly

4 green peppers, cored, de-seeded and finely chopped
1 red pepper, cored, de-seeded and chopped
250 ml (1 cup) apple cider vinegar
750 g sugar
2.5 ml (½ tsp) salt
Juice of 2 lemons

Place all the ingredients in a saucepan and bring to the boil. Cook slowly as for any other chutney until the mixture thickens. Bottle and store. This keeps very well for two or three months. **MAKES 600 ML**

GREEN TOMATO PICKLE

5 kg green tomatoes, finely sliced
6 large onions, cut into rings

BRINE
250 ml (1 cup) salt
Water

CHUTNEY
2.25 litres (9 cups) boiling water
5 ml (1 tsp) celery salt
10 ml (2 tsp) ground cinnamon
1 kg sugar
1 x 100 g box of pickling spice
750 ml (3 cups) white vinegar
25 ml (5 tsp) mustard seeds (optional)

The day before: Soak the tomatoes and onions overnight in a brine made from the salt and sufficient water to cover them.

Next day: Drain the tomatoes and onions. Cover with the boiling water and drain again. Add celery salt, cinnamon, sugar, pickling spice, vinegar and mustard seeds. Bring the mixture to the boil and cook slowly for about 1 hour, stirring frequently. Pour into sterilized bottles and seal while hot.

Note: This is a useful recipe to have when the frost catches the tomato crop and you're left with burned tomato plants and hundreds of green tomatoes. **MAKES ABOUT 4 LARGE PRESERVING JARS (THE OLD 1 LB CONSOL JAR)**

QUICK AND EASY BEETROOT CHUTNEY

750 ml (3 cups) sugar
500 ml (2 cups) brown vinegar
2 x 500 ml (4 cups total) cooked, peeled and cubed beetroot
2 large onions, finely chopped
15 ml (1 Tbsp) curry powder
5 ml (1 tsp) salt
50–75 ml (3–5 Tbsp) cornflour mixed to a paste with a little water

Place the sugar and vinegar in a saucepan and heat slowly, stirring until the sugar has dissolved. Bring to the boil. Once the mixture boils, add the beetroot and onions and simmer for 10 minutes. Add the curry powder and salt and continue simmering for 10 minutes. Stir in the cornflour and allow to thicken. Pour into sterilized bottles while hot. **MAKES ABOUT 2 X 500 ML JARS**

CURRIED CUCUMBERS

250 ml (1 cup) water
1 kg English cucumbers, halved lengthways and thinly sliced
500 g onions, thinly sliced and halved
5 ml (1 tsp) salt
250 ml (1 cup) sugar
500 ml (2 cups) white vinegar
30 ml (2 Tbsp) curry powder
10 ml (2 tsp) mustard powder
60 ml (4 Tbsp) cornflour mixed to a paste with a little water

Bring the water to the boil and cook the cucumbers and onions for 10 minutes. Add salt and sugar and simmer slowly until the sugar has dissolved. Add the rest of the ingredients and boil the mixture until it thickens. Pour into sterilized bottles while hot. **MAKES ABOUT 3 X 500 ML JARS**

Summer Survives in Karoo Farm Pantries

Canned fruit and vegetables are a feature of the country kitchen. In Footprints in the Karoo, *Joan Southey mentions how envious she was of the row upon row of bottles on her neighbour's pantry shelves. 'Halved peaches overlapped each other snugly in perfect symmetry, nestling in syrup, as did the apricots; deep red plums jostled one another like golf balls in their thick sweet juice. Bottles of perfectly sliced green beans as well as glowing ruby beetroot, packed in salted water, were beautiful to behold. Rows of jams, jellies and preserves and marmalades all stood side by side neatly displaying a label noting the variety and date of bottling.' A kitchen pantry exactly like this one left German tourists quite awestruck at Gannakraal Guest Farm near Nelspoort. Shelves of every kind of fruit and vegetable, all neatly bottled, stretched from floor to ceiling, alongside freezers filled with venison, chicken and spinach pies.*

The Coffee House and old filling station, Matjiesfontein.

Cheese

World-class cheese puts Prince Albert on the map

In 1850 when Robert Gray, first Bishop of Cape Town, set off on a journey to the Karoo, his wife, Sophy, packed a good supply of Battley's opium for his headaches, as well as 'a few bottles of wine, some tins of soup, meat and cheese'. Little could she know that a century and a half later cheese would put the Karoo on the world map. In 2002 a full-flavoured, well-matured hard cheese made in Prince Albert walked off with top honours at the South African Farm-Style Cheese Championships run by the National Dairy Institute at Irene. Known as Parma Prince and produced by Gay's Guernsey Dairy, it won first prize in the Italian-style cheese section and was also given a special award as an exceptional cheese. Many of Gay's other cheeses are also winners. They make a well-matured, strong-flavoured Gouda-style cheese known as Prince Albert Royal. It has a distinctive blue wax covering and is served on the Blue Train and Rovos Rail. It has taken top honours at local as well as international cheese shows.

CHEESE PUFFS

250 ml (1 cup) grated Cheddar cheese
5 ml (1 tsp) butter
10 ml (2 tsp) baking powder
250 ml (1 cup) cake flour
Salt and freshly ground black pepper to taste
1 egg
A little milk
Cayenne pepper for sprinkling

Preheat the oven to 220 °C. Mash the grated cheese with the butter. Add the dry ingredients, season and mix well. Beat the egg and add to the mixture. Rinse the egg bowl with milk and add – the mixture must not be too wet. Place teaspoonfuls onto a greased baking sheet and sprinkle lightly with cayenne pepper. Bake for 10 minutes in the oven until golden brown Slice and butter. Serve either hot or cold. **MAKES 12**

Note: Chopped garlic chives or 50 ml (just over 3 Tbsp) chopped crisply fried bacon can be added to vary the flavour.

VERSATILE CHEESE SAUCE

1 thick slice white bread, crusts removed
750 ml–1 litre (3–4 cups) milk
Juice of ½ small lemon
Good pinch of salt
2.5 ml (½ tsp) cayenne pepper
5 ml (1 tsp) paprika
60–125 ml (¼ –½ cup) oil for frying
1 large onion, finely chopped
6 cloves garlic, crushed
3 eggs, beaten
250 ml (1 cup) grated Cheddar cheese (slightly more can be used if desired)

Soak the bread in milk made sour with lemon juice and seasoned with salt, cayenne pepper and paprika. Heat the oil in a pan and fry the onion and garlic until just softened. Add the milk mixture and stir until mixed with the oil. Remove from the heat and let it cool slightly. Add the beaten eggs. Return to the heat. Slowly bring to the boil, while stirring continuously. Remove from the heat and stir in the cheese. Stir until the cheese is melted. Allow to cool. Beat with an electric mixer to smooth away any lumps. **MAKES 1 LITRE**

Note: This sauce originated in Peru, where they pour it over cold sweet potatoes. It also makes a delicious cold sauce for potatoes and a hot sauce for chicken.

CHEESE FRUIT ROLL

250 ml (1 cup) mixed glacé fruit, chopped
45 ml (3 Tbsp) port
250 g (1 tub) smooth cream cheese
125 ml (½ cup) grated Cheddar cheese
5 ml (1 tsp) grated lemon peel
190 ml (¾ cup) poppy seeds

Place the fruit in a bowl. Pour over the port and leave to stand for a few hours. Mix the cheeses and lemon peel together and leave to stand for at least 1 hour. Mix the fruit and cheese mixtures well together. Roll out into a long sausage and then roll in the poppy seeds. Refrigerate for 24 hours. Using a sharp knife, cut into slices and serve with biscuits and cocktails. **SERVES 6–8**

CHEESE TERRINE

350 g butter, softened
45 ml (3 Tbsp) cream cheese with herbs
30 ml (2 Tbsp) chopped fresh parsley
45 ml (3 Tbsp) brandy
Salt and freshly ground black pepper to taste
150 g mozzarella-type cheese, finely grated
150 g (just over ½ tub) smooth cottage cheese
2 cloves garlic, crushed
7.5 ml (1½ tsp) paprika
250 g Queen Vic/Regal or any other strong-flavoured cheese, thinly sliced
15 ml (1 Tbsp) finely grated Parma Prince or Parmesan-type cheese
Sprigs of parsley for garnishing

Using a hand whisk or wooden spoon, cream the butter until soft. Divide into three. Place one-third of the butter in a glass bowl, add the cream cheese with herbs, parsley, half the brandy, salt and pepper to taste and mix well. Place in the refrigerator to rest. Then, grate the mozzarella cheese finely; add the smooth cottage cheese, the garlic and the rest of the brandy. Season to taste. Place in the refrigerator to rest. Place the remaining two-thirds of the butter in a glass bowl, add the paprika and mix well. Grease or line a small loaf pan, 15 cm x 8 cm x 8 cm, with a little butter. Place a layer of strong-flavoured cheese slices on the bottom, overlapping slightly to form a compact base. Spoon the herb cheese mixture onto this and, using a spatula, carefully spread it out over the base. Cover this with another layer of strong-flavoured cheese slices. Spoon the paprika butter onto this and smooth out and sprinkle with the Parmesan. Top this with another layer of strong-flavoured cheese slices, and spoon the mozzarella mixture onto this and smooth out. Finish with a final layer of strong-flavoured cheese slices, overlapping to ensure a firm topping. Place a weight on top and refrigerate overnight to set well and allow the flavours to develop. To serve, slide a knife around the edges, turn out onto a suitable plate and cut into slices using a sharp knife. Decorate with sprigs of parsley. **SERVES 6–8**

Note: The cheeses used in this recipe come from Gay van Hasselt's dairy in Prince Albert.

Festivals

Celebrate the foods of the Karoo

The Karoo is the place to rest, relax and unwind. It's a place where you can reward yourself for a year's hard work, where you can explore, drink in fresh air (and some excellent wines) and treat yourself to quality time and taste treats. Throughout the Karoo the special cuisine of the region is celebrated at a series of interesting small town festivals, some of which have become quite famous over the years.

And then there's a superb string of wine and brandy cellars all along Route 62 from Montagu to the Eastern Cape. A good time to explore these would be after attending one of the special food and wine festivals held at places such as Robertson, Montagu or McGregor, the latter hosting a delightful annual **Country Tastes Festival** on the last Saturday of August each year. Started in 2003 this festival was designed to 'please the eye and soothe the soul'. It offers 'delectable tastes of country fare specific to McGregor and tempting tastes of wines of the beautifully scenic Robertson valley', say the organisers. McGregor also has an annual **Apricot Festival** on the last Saturday of November to celebrate the apricot harvest.

Among the best-known small town festivals is perhaps the Prince Albert Festival, which started out as **The Olive Festival**. It brings people from across South Africa and beyond its borders to the village annually in search of excellent olives and olive products. This festival celebrates the cultural heritage of the village and its surrounds and includes many trips into the district, the Swartberg Mountains and to Gamkaskloof (Die Hel) so that visitors can explore the ecology, natural wonders, an old gold mine, San art, and Anglo-Boer War sites. The festival grew out of the town's olive industry.

Olive growing in the Prince Albert area dates back to the 1970s, when Jan du Preez planted about 100 olive trees on his farm Sandvlakte. They did well. Then, in the 1980s, Jan Bothma started planting Manzanilla and Mission varieties on Swartrivier for processing and Leccino for oil. All varieties flourished because the climate in that part of the Karoo favours olives. Now over 80 tons are harvested annually. Green, black and half-ripe olives are processed for bottling, but a variety of other products are also available. These include dried black olives, spiced olives, green and black olive paste, cold-pressed extra virgin oil and olive soap. The success of Swartrivier products led to a mushrooming interest in olives and these days most Prince Albert residents make a variety of olive-based products. And so do many others as far afield as Beaufort West, where the local school produces excellent olive oil and a farm near Nelspoort is also a producer of superb olive products. During the **Prince Albert Festival** freshly baked olive bread is a speciality and olive dishes appear on every guesthouse and restaurant menu. Games and events are structured around the olives and perhaps the one that gets the greatest laughs is the Olive Spitting Competition.

Prince Albert also has a top-class cheese farm and some well-known wines. An excellent sweet wine, Soet Karoo, is produced by Herman and Susan Perholdt at a venue in the town's main street. Visitors are encouraged to call at all these venues for tastings. The festival is usually held just before Easter so that visitors can also take in the famous **Klein Karoo Kunstefees** in Oudtshoorn. Here again, in addition to the shows, which are usually sold out well in advance, the emphasis is on fun and local foods, mostly with an ostrich flavour.

An annual German **Oktoberfest** is also held in Prince Albert. This began in 2002 to honour Queen Victoria's beloved husband, Prince Albert of Saxe Coburg-Gotha, after whom the town was named, plus the fact that Queen Victoria proposed to him at their third meeting, on 15 October 1839. When visitors ask: 'Why a German festival in a Karoo town with British roots?', the locals answer 'simple'. Prince Albert, the man who stole Queen Victoria's heart was German and he was a fascinating person. He prided himself on being a pillar of moral rectitude. He went to an all-male university and foreswore contact with women. Victoria was bowled over by his 'striking beauty' and felt herself unworthy of him, yet she proposed. (Her superior status made this role reversal necessary.) At first he was not impressed, but he eventually consented after warning her he would not allow himself to be 'corrupted' by her. Many say it was he and not she who was the prude! Albert was a dedicated father and enthusiastic teacher of his nine children. He was the driving force behind the first World Exhibition in 1851 and he created the Crystal Palace where it was held. He also developed London's sewerage system and was an ardent student of architecture and music. He wrote Queen Victoria's speeches and it was he who suggested the introduction of the Victoria Cross, Britain's highest military award for bravery.

On the menu at the Oktoberfest visitors will find eisbein, sauerkraut and draught beer as well as kassler, bockwurst, and kartoffeln, a variety of German sausages and plenty of typical Karoo braaivleis and salads. There is also much traditional German and oom-pah-pah music. Normally the local St John's Anglican Church's **Flower Festival** is also held in October. It's designed to welcome spring and has a more English bill of fare.

Somerset East has a **Biltong Festival**. Started in 1991 this was the brainchild of Willem de Klerk, a farmer from Bedford, the Swaershoek Farmer's Union and the local Chamber of Commerce. De Klerk managed to rally a committee of stakeholders to co-ordinate the festival and he also motivated nature conservation, tourism groups and the local municipality to participate. Castle Lager sponsored the seventeenth festival, held in July 2007, so the Blue Crane Route Municipality allowed them naming rights, and thus the **Castle Lager Eastern Cape Biltong Festival** was born.

Over the years the theme of the festival has changed from simply portraying typical Karoo life and it has become a fun music festival with a large craft market. It attracts entertainers, solo artists and choirs, as well as crafters from across the country. InterCape provides an open-topped 'Fun Bus' complete with a well-known celebrity to act as commentator and 'guide'. The bus takes festival-goers on tours of Somerset East. For the more adventurous there are helicopter flights and camel rides. And, as with most small town festivals, local dishes and taste treats are in great demand.

Calitzdorp's **Port Festival**, which started in 1992, is also still going strong. It takes place every two years in July and affords visitors every opportunity to find out all about the town's world famous port. Fun and fresh air are the main themes and there are daily wine tasting tours and cellar crawls by tractor. There are also formal port tasting outings and there is usually a symposium on wine, port or some aspect of wine farming and production for enthusiasts to attend. There are art exhibitions, sports and a series of stalls with useful and unusual items for sale. Craft demonstrations are well attended and so are cooking demonstrations, particularly those using the local wines and ports. Also high on the popularity stakes are such special events as vine pruning and scarecrow building competitions. Again there are several fun events, such as cork spitting and barrel rolling. This is a festival which concentrates on fun, food, wine and port for a full three or four days.

Calvinia's **Annual Hantam Meat Festival** takes place in August. This popular festival, established to promote sheep farming and meat products, includes sheep shearing and whip-plaiting competitions and demonstrations on how to cut up a carcass, de-bone meat and make soap. There is also a mock farmyard, which is great fun for the children. Festivities begin with a gala ball at which the festival queen is crowned. Then there is a parade of veteran cars, drum majorettes and a competition for the best slaughter lamb (on the hoof). There is always a wide range of stalls and some offer irresistible, traditional taste treats such as offal, baked sheep's head, liver sausage, *skilpadjies*, mutton neck, braaied tails, chops, *wors* (sausage), sosaties, potjiekos and kliprib. The *kuierkafee* (café for visitors) encourages people to sit, chat and catch up on the news over a cup of tea or coffee with some delicious accompaniments. Well-known artists and local bands entertain visitors.

The Karoo has many other festivals and events to encourage tourists to visit and share the ambience and foods of the area. Among these is the Laingsburg 80 km Ultra Marathon, usually run in September. Keen long-distance runners consider this a training ground for the Comrades. Their supporters come to enjoy the *lekker local kos* (delicious local food) in the pristine natural environments that surround the town.

**FOR MORE INFORMATION
ON THE KAROO'S FESTIVALS:**
McGregor: Tel. (023) 625-2954 or
    e-mail mcgregortour@telkomsa.net
Prince Albert: Tel. (023) 541-1366 or
    e-mail princealberttourism@intekom.co.za
Blue Crane Route: Tel. (042) 243-1333 or
    e-mail bcrm.tourism@lgnet.org.za
Calitzdorp: Tel. (044) 213-3775 or
    e-mail calitzdorpinfo@telkomsa.net
Calvinia: E-mail maxie@hantam.co.za
ABSA KKNK: Tel. (044) 203-8600 or
    e-mail info@kknk.co.za

Contributors

Fairleigh Burher: pp.75 (top), 137 (bottom); **Calitzdorp**: pp. 45, 126 (top), 127, 143 (third); **Elmien de Ridder and Elzona Deetlefs**: p. 84 (middle); **Tersia de Wit**: pp. 83, 84 (bottom), 85, 86, 87 (top and bottom), 101 (top); **Helena du Toit**: p. 130 (bottom); **Deanise Edwards**: pp. 16 (top), 19 (left), 39, 40 (top), 47, 72, 104 (bottom), 114 (top and bottom), 135; **Deanise Edwards/Helene Mulder**: p. 18; **Late Anna Estherhuizen (Williston Museum)**: p. 138 (top); **Belinda Gordon**: pp. 29 (bottom), 32 (top), 111 (middle), 154 (top and bottom); **Diana Greathead**: p. 90 (bottom); **Greeff Heydenrych**: pp. 63 (top), 64 (top and bottom), 66, 67; **Netta Hollander**: p. 104 (middle); **Maxie Hugo**: pp. 103 (bottom), 138 (box), 141 (middle), 147 (bottom left); **Kobie Jeppe**: pp. 30 (top), 33 (top), 40 (bottom), 48 (top and bottom), 51 (top and bottom), 55 (top), 99, 110, 143 (top); **Kotie Jonkers**: p. 104 (top); **Ray Kibur**: p. 16 (bottom); **Late Kittie Krugel (Williston Museum)**: p. 147 (top right); **Anita Langner**: p. 102 (top); **Danie Langner**: p. 94 (middle); **Late Kosie le Roux (Williston Museum)**: p. 75 (bottom); **Late Tannie Anny Louw (Williston Museum)**: p. 60 (top); **May Louw**: p. 19 (right); **Martie Lund**: pp. 21, 37; **Johanna Luttig**: pp. 26, 32, 68 (top), 94 (top), 98 (bottom), 111 (top), 125 (middle), 130 (middle); **Late Bonnie Mahlo (Williston Museum)**: p. 30 (top); **Elna Marais**: pp. 139, 155 (top); **Late Grieta Marais (Williston Museum)**: pp. 134 (bottom), 138 (middle); **Johan Marais**: p. 56; **Late Lena Marais (Williston Museum)**: p. 126 (bottom); **Pat Marincowitz**: pp. 33 (box), 120 (box); **Amanda Mathee**: p. 52 (top); **Late Jack Mulder (Williston Museum)**: p. 60 (bottom); **Ann Murray**: pp. 52 (bottom), 61, 63 (bottom), 90 (top); **Ria Oosthuizen**: pp. 88, 89, 107 (bottom), 113 (bottom), 125 (top), 141 (bottom), 144 (left); **Peter Pankhurst**: p. 97; **Charlotte Roux**: p. 68 (bottom); **Mary Sandock**: p. 20 (box); **Dr Taffy Shearing**: p. 80 (box); **Elsie Smuts**: pp. 121 (bottom), 133 (top and bottom); **Penny Southey**: pp. 29 (top), 59, 105; **Johanna Spann**: pp. 36, 120 (top), 147 (bottom right), 148 (top left), 152 (middle and bottom); **Hilary Steven Jennings**: pp. 107 (top), 111 (bottom), 123, 130 (top), 137 (top), 141 (top), 142, 143 (second), 147 (top left), 148 (bottom left), 148 (right), 152 (top); **May Taylor**: p. 20 (bottom); **Gudrun Toelstede**: p.118; **Ann Louise van der Colff**: p. 113 (middle); **Elsa van Schalkwyk**: pp. 32 (box), 98 (top), 101 (bottom), 106, 122 (top), 143 (bottom); **Andre Viviers**: p. 94 (bottom); **Yvonne Weiss**: p. 76 (bottom); **Lorna Willis**: pp. 74, 122 (bottom); **May Willis**: pp. 43 (top), 76 (top), 80 (top), 149 (top), 151 (top); **Rose Willis**: pp. 22, 79, 103 (top), 134 (top), 144 (right), 151 (middle and bottom), 155 (bottom); **Rose Willis (from Granny's cookbook)**: pp. 34, 44 (bottom); **Rose Willis (from Madeline Kriek)**: pp. 27, 43 (bottom), 125 (bottom); **Rose Willis (from Wally Kriek)**: p. 102; **Rose Willis (from Sheila Young)**: p. 149 (bottom); **Derek Wright**: pp. 44 (top), 55 (bottom), 113 (top).

Bibliography

Butler, Guy. *Tales from the Old Karoo*, A D Donker (Pty) Limited, 1989.

Coetzee, Renata. *The South African Culinary Tradition*, C. Struik, 1977.

Cumming, Roualeuyn Gordon (of Altyre). *Five Years of a Hunter's Life in the Far Interior of South Africa*, 1850.

Five Years' Adventures in the Far Interior of South Africa, with notices of the Native Tribes and Savage Animals, John Murray, London, 1904.

De Mist, Jonkvrou Augusta Uitenhage. *Diary of a Journey to the Cape and Interior of Africa*, A A Balkema, Cape Town.

Delegorgue, Adolphe. *Travels in Southern Africa*.

Faull, Leslie; Heard, Vida and Shearing, Diana (eds). *Bread, Buns/Cakes and Cookies*, Books of Africa, 1970.

Graaff Reinet – The Gem of the Karoo, Official Guide, Spandau Boekhandel.

Green, Lawrence G. *Land of the Afternoon*, Howard Timmins, 1949.

Karoo, Howard Timmins, 1955.

Lucas, T C. *Camp Life and Sport in South Africa*.

Martin, Annie. *Home Life on an Ostrich Farm*, George Philip and Son, London, 1891.

Minnaar, Lynne; Reynolds, Annatjie and Neethling, Albé. *Karoo Venison*, 2003.

O'Haire, Rev. James. *Recollections of Twelve Years in South Africa 1863–1875*, James Duffy and Sons, Dublin, 1883.

Palmer, Eve. *Return to Camdeboo – A Century's Karoo Foods and Flavours*, Tafelberg Publishers, Cape Town, 1992.

The Plains of Camdeboo, Jonathan Ball Publishers, 1993.

Pringle, Thomas; Wahl, John Robert (ed.). *Poems Illustrative of South Africa*, C. Struik, 1970.

Skead, C J. *Historical Mammal Incidence in the Cape Province*, Volume 1, The Western and Northern Cape, Department of Nature and Environmental Conservation of the Cape of Good Hope, 1980.

Southey, Joan. *Footprints in the Karoo – a Story of Farming Life*, Jonathan Ball, 1990.

The Beaufort West Courier. Various issues.

The Guide To South Africa For The Use Of Tourists, Sportsmen, Invalids And Settlers, 1896–97 edition.

Van As, Norma. *A Small World – The Descendants of Charles Webber*, Norma van As, 1981.

Van der Post, Laurens. *A Mantis Carol*, The Hogarth Press, London, 1975.

Van Rensburg, S W J. *From The Horse's Mouth – The Story of South Africa's Veteran Vet*, Van Schaik, 1983.

Van Zyl, Dine. *Potjiekos*, Saaiman and Weber, 1983.

Vivier, W G H and S. Hooyvlakte – *Die verhaal van Beaufort-Wes 1818–1968*, Nasionale Boekhandel, 1969.

Wessels, Elria (ed.). *Boerespyse – resepte en kospraatjies van die Anglo-Boereoorlog*, the War Museum of the Boer Republics, Bloemfontein, 1994.

Recipe Index

Page numbers in *italics* indicate photographs.